SOMETIMES YOU HAVE TO EAT A CRAP SANDWICH

A collection of short essays to help improve your career mileage

DON FESH

Critique Partner & Developmental Editor: Katie Bruce
Cover Design By Champagne Book Design

SOMETIMES YOU HAVE TO EAT A CRAP SANDWICH

A collection of short essays to help improve your career mileage

(including mistakes I've made, but you don't have to)

A Book By: DON FESH

CONTENTS

If you find yourself eating a crap sandwich you are
allowed to try something else on the menu…
or consider changing restaurants.

INTRODUCTION

S O, WHY READ A BOOK ABOUT AN AVERAGE GUY INSTEAD OF AN extraordinary person who went on to become CEO of a Fortune 500 company and changed the world? The reason you read this book is because the odds are a lot more likely you will follow a typical career path like me than that of an iconic CEO. This doesn't mean you shouldn't aspire to be iconic; it's just that a lot of things have to happen to elevate to that level—not only at large companies, but at medium and small ones too. If you want pure inspiration about someone who overcame insurmountable odds or used their immense genius and made it big, this isn't the book for you. If you want to follow the path of someone who did OK, but probably could have done better if they had taken more calculated risks, knew what career-hindering warning signs to look for, and had the luxury of hindsight that would have evoked different actions, this may be the book for you. If you are in your 20's, 30's or early 40's, I hope reading this helps you avoid some of the pitfalls I experienced... and helps you realize when you are in a career hole, and how to stop digging it deeper.

Lacking a mentor or an advocate at places I worked required me to figure things out on my own—I'm not complaining, but if I had some idea of how to navigate a few situations a little differently, I may have chosen an alternate fork in my career path, leading me in a more successful direction. If you are in your late 40's & 50's, a lot of this content may resonate with you, and may motivate you to do something a little different to finish your career strong instead of limping or dragging yourself to the finish line.

Of course, this is only one person's experience and perspective, so it may have detractors and critics, but I can only share what I know. Not everyone is going to agree with everything written—if you read something that makes good sense to you, use it. If something sounds like terrible advice, ignore it. I hope you enjoy the book; find it entertaining, a little humorous and hopefully beneficial in helping you navigate your career.

CHAPTER 1

Wow, Am I Lucky...

A S YOU READ THIS BOOK THERE ARE GOING TO BE TIMES WHERE what I say comes across as complaining. OK, to be clear, I am definitely complaining, but please know that I absolutely understand how fortunate I am to have been born in the United States, truly the land of opportunity.

I had so many things going for me that I really have no room to complain about anything. I always had a roof over my head, a full belly and a safe place to live. Even though I grew up in a blue-collar household in an area and time where layoffs were a regular occurrence and both parents had to work to make sure their kids had food and clothing, I never felt desperate or sad.

Maybe wearing hand me down clothes and living a more humble life drove me to do better than what I knew growing up, but it also may have limited me once I thought I had "achieved enough" ...not really sure, but that would require a deeper, more philosophical dive than I'm interested in doing.

It's not like I've been a failure; I'm sure there are many people that would envy the opportunities and career I've had. I just believe that with a few different decisions I could have achieved what I achieved sooner, and maybe even achieved more than I did. As you read, you will notice that I assign partial responsibility of some of my career stalls at different

1

companies to what I believe were poor leaders. I do believe that this assessment is fair and emphasizes the importance of good leadership, but also know that I place the majority of responsibility on myself for not taking action to change my situation—no one forced me to work anywhere or continue to report to anyone—those were my choices.

I also share suggestions throughout—suggestions that I didn't always follow or live by. I did eventually grow into them, but these are things I learned to do with experience and with 20/20 hindsight, are what I would do now. The other thing to understand as you read this is that my career has been overwhelmingly positive, the people I worked with terrific, and the work itself challenging and interesting. Many of the examples I provide are the opposite of that description, which was done because it's easy to handle the routine stuff—it's harder to understand how to handle the odd-ball things that can surprise you. As an FYI, this book is not written chronologically; it's just examples taken from different points in my life and career.

Other than wanting to share some of my experiences with the hope that others may benefit from them, there was no additional underlying motivation to write this beyond what I've already stated. Personally, I'm in a good place spiritually, philosophically, physically and financially... so, no axe to grind.

Thanks for taking the time to read my short stories. I hope they are helpful, or at a minimum entertaining.

If you enjoy what you read, and are comfortable doing so, please feel free to share this with others. I'm only "marketing" this book through organic channels, so word of mouth is both helpful and appreciated.

To quote George Santayana: "those who cannot learn from history are doomed to repeat it."

CHAPTER 2

I Knew I Was in a Hole... and How I Stopped Digging

Alternate chapter title:
Some Background and a Walk Down My Meandering
Path of Sacrifice and Motivation That Led Me to College

WORKED A LOT OF INTERESTING JOBS IN MY YOUTH, SOME OF which I still half-joke have certainly shortened my life by 10 years. For example, a long, long time ago in a peninsula state far, far away... while working at a power plant, I stepped into something called a "perc pond" which is short for percolation pond, and that was somehow allowed to be on this property, near a river no less. It's basically a place where hazardous chemicals were dumped into a big hole and allowed to percolate through a filtering process into the ground (or so I think. I really don't know, as I'm not a chemist, but it was basically a thick, noxious pool of chemical sludge). When I stepped into it, or as I recall, was actually pushed into the pond by someone who I believe to be a sociopath (but I'm getting off topic...back to the pond) as I "stepped" into it, I was fortunately able to catch my balance and have only one foot and half of my leg go in. It was thick like quicksand and the suction pulled my big rubber boot off, leaving one foot and leg covered with a special blend of thick, creamy & gritty toxic soup. I found my way back to the showers as quickly as I could and scrubbed myself down like

3

I was just exposed to radiation. As far as I know, I did not have any negative long-term complications, and on the plus side, the extra toe that later grew out of the side of my foot is a fun conversation starter at the beach.

On another occasion at that plant, I remember being in a 13-story boiler (I think it was 13) and my job was to "clean the slopes" of the boiler where a bunch of slag buildup occurs around the 2nd story level. I was in there for about an hour wearing my safety harness and respirator when a supervisor called me over from the fresh air side of the boiler. Through the little hole I crawled in, they reached in and unscrewed the respirator cartridges I was wearing on my mask and screwed two new ones on and said the following: "you are wearing purple cartridges, and you should be wearing green ones." WHAT? So, what exactly was I breathing in for the last 60 minutes that the purple cartridges were unable to filter?

If that wasn't enough, I also had the pleasure of crawling around in an area called "the void" to clean up some sort of toxic debris mixed with fiberglass. Another fun activity was using a fire hose to clean out a smokestack. The dripping water from the tall stack during this experience was full of some chemical that made my lips and face completely numb—but no worries, feeling returned in about 12 hours. I also got to "shoot condensers" in something called a water box, worked under the ocean in a tube called a plenum, on top of a cooling tower, and had the wonderful experience of crawling into something called a heat exchange pipe. This was my specialty; not due to any specialized training or skill, but rather because I was skinny and could fit. I would be outfitted with rain gear, handed a scraping tool (to take off barnacles) and shoved into a narrow 50ish foot long pipe headfirst. For "safety" I had a rope tied to one of my ankles (which I quadruple knotted). When reaching the end or a turn in the pipe, I would have to send a signal for the guy on the outside of the pipe to tug on the rope to pull me out. None of these things were something you looked forward to, and all were as awful as they sound. I knew I was in a hole and needed to stop digging. The only silver lining is that this was incredible motivation for me to consider college.

Other college-motivating jobs before I started my career at the local Junior College (JC) included working in the warehouse at an electrical supply company. Occasionally, this job saw me loading wire trucks or driving to "the dump," where during one trip over a 6-mile bridge, the hood of the truck popped up and made it so I couldn't see the road. With no emergency lanes to pull over into, I had to drive slowly with my head out the window until I got to the end…but again, I digress. On a good day, this job also had me occasionally doing yard work for the owner of the company. Other jobs had me working on an assembly line (think Lucy and Ethel at the chocolate factory), in a call center, doing oil changes, at a music and video store back when such places existed, and in a clean room assembling surgical kits. By the way, I lasted all of 2 days on the assembly line. Being someone who gets dizzy watching special effects during a movie and struggles being a passenger in a car, it was probably not the best career move. The company tried to find me a spot, and on the second day they put me in the "cold room" which was just a huge freezer. The food we were making on the assembly line was frozen, so my job was driving the forklift in the freezer. So, here I was living in Florida, bundled in a parka so I didn't freeze to death in the cold room.

…Off to College

Out of the Hole: Although I had some transferable credits from attending a community college in Pennsylvania, I was still going to have a long 2 year journey through the Junior College in Florida, mostly because I couldn't afford to attend full-time and had to work to earn money to pay for school. It was more expensive than it should have been as I was considered "out of state" and wouldn't be considered "in state" for a break on tuition costs for 2 years—I think they called it establishing residency. What was funny is that if I tried to go back to Pennsylvania, I would be considered "out of state" there, as well. So, now I have no state—what a mess. Quick lesson: take a minute to think things through – no one is going to care that your situation seems unfair.

While in school, I worked hard to get in and out as quickly as I could. I felt like I had some ground to make up. Even though I was only 22-23, many young people my age were already finishing college, and here I was still trying to get started. I remember having a couple of inspirational instructors and some real duds. The duds just showed up to make some money as part of a side hustle, not called that back then, but that's basically what it was. The inspirational professors were usually the ones excited to share knowledge and were happy to see someone grasp a new concept. It was these instructors who made me want to attend class.

This is also about the time when I figured out that doing the assignments, reading the textbook and showing up for class would just about guarantee a passing grade, if not better. All my academic experience up until this point was passive at best. I don't remember reading many of the assignments in high school, and I also missed a lot of school—I recall it just boring me, so I wouldn't go. My first experience at the Pennsylvania community college had me playing on the soccer team, so hanging out with the team and traveling to games was by far more fun than the school work. I did have incentive however—I knew to stay on the team I had to attend classes and maintain a minimum passing GPA.

It took a while to climb out of the hole:

I finally completed my 2 years at JC and transferred to my four-year institution. My previous jobs paid little to nothing, plus I was paying for school, so saving was difficult. But I was able to squirrel a little away and was glad to no longer feel like I was in a hole, which was, and always is a good feeling.

Fortunately, I also qualified for some student loans and a pretty minimal grant, which was just enough to allow me to attend school and rent a cheap apartment (that I could only afford by splitting costs with a roommate). The apartment backed up to a fire station and bordered on a main road with a railroad track running on the side of it—it was quite an adventure to be woken up nightly by either fire sirens, a train or drunk drivers speeding down the road. We also had an upstairs neighbor that worked a late shift and would come home to take a bath every night around 3:00 AM—the bathroom was directly above my room. The neighbor I shared a wall with had a bird that talked all day while they were at work. Great fun. Apparently, I was still in a hole…less deep, but still a hole. Back to school—fortunately, my experience from JC taught me to go to class and to read the assignments. I also started to get involved with clubs and activities, which was not a natural thing for me to do (other than sports). I tried a club in high school once…not really a club, but student council. I remember being allowed out of class to attend the meetings, but I usually just got out of class and went to do something else. Funny, I still don't care for politics. Anyway, I burned a couple of years and now I wanted to embrace and enjoy the college experience.

While in college I had a few jobs to help make ends meet. Through persistence and a little badgering, I obtained two internships with a couple of large well-known companies. This is when I was introduced to "Corporate America" and saw how a professional corporate path could provide financial security.

Now that I knew the secret to school was doing the assigned work, I turned into an impressive student…even made The Dean's List. I graduated with a high GPA, and now it was time to look for a job. Unfortunately, this was during a downturn in the economy and jobs were difficult to come by, but I ultimately found one working for a trucking company. I took the job but felt like I was right back where I had left off. Here I had transformed myself into a model student, was now seen as someone very likely to succeed, and yet I ended up doing manual labor again. If that wasn't bad enough, on busy days supervisors (like me) also had to "work the belt" which was basically an assembly line of packages. This was the same thing that I did years before that had inspired me to go to college. Don't get me wrong, there is nothing wrong with manual labor; but I've done that, and now wanted something different. My shallow hole just got deeper again. How do I stop digging now?

I started to look for other jobs and fortunately found a role that fit nicely with what I did as an intern, so I landed a job with a municipality as a purchasing manager. Even more fortunate, the job was in a city near family, so I had a support system available if needed. I had an office, wore a tie every day, had staff and was contributing and making decisions that felt important. Funny story, I bought new shirts and pants for my new professional job (which basically broke the bank for me) and the first time I washed all the shirts together I discovered that I had left a pen in one of the pockets and got ink on every new shirt. Sigh. I remember my mother and I working to take the stains out… as I recall, hairspray somehow works well to remove ink from fabric. Such a small bump in the road, but it seemed like such a big deal at the time. The new job was OK, and I met some nice people. I learned how to deal with difficult employees and managers and also started to define my management and leadership style.

I realized pretty quickly, however, that I still wanted more, as after a year or so of doing this it became pretty routine. I knew a Master's Degree could open additional doors, so I started to look at programs and tried to figure out how I was going to pay for a Master's Degree while still earning a living. Again, through persistence, I found a job at an accredited University that was similar to what I was currently doing. I applied for and landed that job, with one of the employee benefits being free tuition. I had to move out of state, and the job was not exactly glamourous, but I got to work on a lot of big projects and gained new experience— and it came with a free MBA. Well, mostly free—the second year of the program the government decided to tax the "value" of the classes I was getting for free as income—thanks, government!

For two years I worked all day, went to school at night and studied every spare minute I had. Oh, and my girlfriend lived 4.5 hours away, and I would drive to see her every other weekend, and she to see me on alternating weekends. During these trips to visit her, I would listen to class notes I recorded and play them back during my drive - it seemed like a good way to learn my academic material (an early version of a podcast… with only one listener). Like many people, I don't love my voice. I wasn't a professional voice over person, so the tapes were less than dynamic; in fact, they were pretty monotone. I remember once lulling myself to sleep with the recordings and I just about crashed. Good thing the side of the road had some rumble strips that woke me up. After this incident, I thought about selling the recordings as sleep aids, but never did (missed opportunity). To make sure I didn't fall asleep again, I started to try and spice up the recordings a little with some fluctuations of my voice, and would throw in little jokes or say something to myself to keep things interesting. Every once in a while, I would hear something I forgot I had recorded and laugh. I wish I still had those recordings… mostly to help me sleep.

The point of all of this is to show that you can get yourself out of holes and overcome challenging obstacles, but it may require persistence, determination, dedication, and an ability to stay focused and keep moving forward. I understood it came with a need to sacrifice time, family, relationships and even salary (I could have made more, but realized an education was important). In the back of my mind, I knew it was worth it; I also believed it would open doors and that no one could ever take my education away from me. Worthwhile things usually require effort—don't ever expect an easy button or hand out.

As I was finishing up my MBA, my girlfriend and I got engaged. She wasn't happy with her job, and I wanted to work somewhere I could grow. The University was a nice place, but it had limited career paths. Together, we targeted a handful of cities, and both agreed we would move when one of us found a great job. She found an exciting role in the Dallas area, so we moved—her with a new career, me with nothing. Once again feeling like I had a lot to offer but nowhere to contribute. How did I end up back in a hole! It took 6 long months, but I found a position with a big healthcare company. I was brought in as an analyst, but was provided opportunities to do side projects related to financials & budgeting, as well as other assignments creating relational databases to track data and create performance related reports. I also found myself working within the IT department, so I learned a lot about the IT side of things. This combined with my business background turned out to make me a pretty good interpreter & liaison between business and IT people.

Within two years that company sold their Texas division. The acquiring company offered me a role in a different city where their HQ was located, and what remained of the old company offered me a role in yet another city working for one of their non-divested areas. We had just moved to Texas, and my now wife had a great job, so I declined both offers. Through a network connection I was fortunate to be able to quickly find a new job at a company that was also positioned within the healthcare space. It was in a small, but fast-growing department, which sounded good to me. I was eager to learn, contribute and grow as the department grew, and hopefully prove my worth along the way. I hadn't noticed it at the time, but this now labeled me as a "healthcare professional."

Missed Opportunity?

I may have missed an opportunity by not relocating again. The company that bought out the Texas division I was working for was public, and they offered discounted stock as well as stock options as part of the compensation package. I'll never know, but I didn't want to dwell on what could have been. Rather, I was going to focus on what was in front of me.

CHAPTER 3

Where Is This Going?

WHEN YOU ARE DOING YOUR JOB, EVEN VERY EARLY IN YOUR career, look to where you want to be and ask yourself: is this position going to help me get there? If the answer is yes, ask yourself how. 2 years of experience doing something you can use as a steppingstone is great, but the same 2 years of experience over a 10-year period of time is not a good thing. If you are not growing in the role, or if the role isn't going to help get you to where you want to be, then you should consider seeking a different path. Life isn't a fairytale and no one is going to come pluck you out of your position because they magically discovered you were smart, nice, and deserving and decided to take a chance on you. The reality is, unless you have been recruited out of a prestigious academic program and/or identified as a fast-track employee, you will likely have to make something happen yourself.

Keep your radar on for when opportunities present themselves... when they do, pounce on those opportunities and make the most of them; it may be your ticket to the next step in your climb to where you want to be. My career is filled with opportunities I didn't take advantage of.

And remember: good work doesn't always speak for itself. I always thought this would be true since it worked this way at smaller companies in more entry level roles and little competition. In a larger company, with a more competitive environment, many people are doing impressive work, so you need to stand out.

Don't worry about what anyone else thinks of you along the way – do what's necessary to be challenged and grow. Be ethical and don't purposefully harm anyone along the way, but you shouldn't feel guilty for offering ideas, being educated, dedicated, and asking for and delivering on opportunities.

It's OK, You Have Time

So, you are in your 20's, maybe early 30's, you've been working for a few years and are making decent money. The company is good, and it looks like you will have room to grow. As you continue to take on additional responsibility you also want to advance in title and pay, and you hear "be patient, it will come". Well, depending on who is telling you this, it may not come, and quite frankly waiting patiently may be foolish. I know you think 5 years, 10 years even 20 years is a long time, but the reality is it's not. It's going to fly by, and before you know it, you're going to be one of the old timers at work…you really will. The music you listen to will seem out of touch with younger people, and they'll be doing things, wearing things, and saying things that will make no sense to you. When you do try to wear some new fashion, you will just look silly, and by the time you hear about the latest popular fad, it will already be out of favor (most likely because old farts like you are now aware of it).

You think this won't happen, but it will. One day you will suddenly realize that you are not seen as young, hip or cool (saying hip and cool shows how out of touch I am). You may feel young because you can keep up with the younger crowd at the gym… then one day you can't. You may try, but your body will resent the attempt. The next day the younger people will do it all over again, but you will need to take a few days off to recover. I'm not going to say my exact age, but there are days after working in the yard, playing tennis or just piddling around the house where it's a struggle to bend over to put on a pair of shoes, assuming I can even find them. When I was in my early to mid-20's, I used to be able to hold a pair of shorts out in front of me and jump into them with both feet at the same time… literally holding the shorts, jumping into the air, and placing both legs into the shorts! The good news is, this was not a skill that ever earned me any money, so losing it wasn't that big of a deal. Just understand some of the things you used to take for granted may no longer be easy. You may also have additional responsibilities like kids or caring for an aging or sick family member. None of this is to say you can't still be awesome at your job and even be better than anyone else, I'm just saying you need to make the most of the time you have; don't be too patient because while you wait for something to happen, others are likely making things happen.

Patience Pays Off…or Does It?

Here is what can happen while you wait patiently for your career to take off: leadership changes, their friends and old colleagues are brought in from the outside, you lose your advocate, and/or the technology your skills are tied to changes. If you wait patiently, something good may happen for you, but don't count on it. While other people have been telling you to "be patient," suddenly 10 years pass and now people say, "they have been in that role for 10 years, they are never going anywhere." If you are overly patient, you will be relocated from the "rising star" box to the "doesn't have a future" box. This can, and will happen—if you let it.

Always expect that you will need to make your own path. You are still allowed to accept assistance along the way, but YOU need to initiate action to generate forward momentum. It's OK to have a little patience while you learn, but once you've mastered what you are doing, stop being patient and look for the next opportunity. Ask to take on new projects or responsibilities that will make you more marketable, either internally or outside the company. If you sit in contentment, everyone around you may move past you.

There is only so much to learn in any given job, and once multiple people know the job, you are no longer as valuable or marketable as you once were. Now you are one of several people who can do X role. Stay on the lookout for some new challenge and when possible, take on something that makes you intellectually curious. If you don't, you will simply find yourself sitting in the same chair, at the same desk, doing the same thing for a long time—wondering what happened. For some, this is OK. There is nothing wrong with being content at something you are good at, and some like the routine and stability a familiar job offers. If you are planning to grow, however, you can't expect it's going to come find you.

Other Thoughts:

You can go from "highly thought of" to "out of favor" overnight depending on which way the prevailing winds are blowing. Definitely leverage your "highly thought of" status while you can. Look for ways to advance, take on exciting assignments, push for promotions, raises, bonuses, stock… whatever is available to you. You may believe that you will always be viewed in this positive and glowing way, and you might, but the odds are against you. At some point you will either become too expensive, be in someone's way, or seen as a threat during a power struggle fought by weak-minded people. Don't get too comfortable, and always be thinking about plan B in case something happens. By the way, never feel guilty about taking advantage of opportunities when you have them, as they can dry up quickly.

CHAPTER 4

Definitely Buy That Expensive Car!

So, NOW THAT YOU HAVE AN IMPRESSIVE SALARY, IT'S TIME TO LET the world know you have arrived by buying that head-turning new car. Unless the company is paying for it, don't do it. The new car makes you feel great... for about a month or two, then it's just transportation. Don't get me wrong, I was in the same boat. I needed a vehicle; my wife needed a vehicle and I wanted a toy to play with (a motorcycle... talk about first world problems). At the time, I really would have loved to have a Porsche and a nice high performance 4-wheel drive truck, as well as a high-end motorcycle. Instead, we went with a Mazda MX5, a Toyota Tacoma and an entry level Kawasaki motorcycle (later changed to a Ducati, but I'm wandering off topic). We were able to get all of them for less than the cost of a single sportscar and have loved all three. Their maintenance costs are also considerably lower; I think we calculated being able to get all 4 tires for the Mazda for less than one high performance tire on the Porsche (or close to it). There is also nowhere we can drive that requires the level of performance built into a high-end sports car.

The truck is my daily driver and I like having it for weekend work like picking up bags of mulch or whatever from the hardware store or nursery – but I don't need a high performance, 4-wheel drive vehicle to do that. And as much as I would have loved a certain European motorcycle,

I got a similar experience for a third of the cost. I asked my wife: do you want a Porsche, or a convertible MX5 + a Tacoma + a Motorcycle + a trip to Europe and the ability to retire earlier than planned. Italy was beautiful.

We also keep our vehicles forever… this may not be right for everyone, but for us it made sense. A high-quality car with regular maintenance can last a long time. As of this writing, I've had my truck for 15+ years and my wife has had her car for 10+. That equates to a lot of years with no vehicle payments. You don't have to buy the cheapest car on the planet, but the point is that there may be lower priced options that still provide the experience you want and are similar to the higher priced option, but will leave you with additional purchasing power and more financial flexibility. If you can buy a Mercedes, BMW, Audi, Porsche… whatever it may be, and not even blink at the cost because you have so much disposable income and savings, it may be perfectly fine to buy that car. If you have to reach to afford it, or think about the cost, you should probably consider something less expensive. I'm not suggesting you shouldn't enjoy the journey of life; just be smart about how much you pay to enjoy it. There is another entire debate & discussion about pre-owned and leasing, but I'll leave that for another day.

To reiterate: definitely enjoy the things that make being alive worthwhile, but be sure you have enough money to last you until you are dead—trust me, you want to end up in the nice nursing home that fluffs your pillow and helps you comb your hair every day… not the one that leaves you sitting in a hallway for hours, forgets to give you your medication, doesn't change your sheets for a month and steals your pudding (mmmmm, pudding!)

CHAPTER 5

You Will Always Have Your Health

If you have always been healthy, you may think you will always be healthy… believing this is a fallacy. In addition to being healthy, I was always able to outwork most of my colleagues… here was my formula:

1   I was good at what I did. I studied, worked hard, practiced my craft, absorbed information… you name it. I wanted to be good at whatever my role was—really good. In order to make any of the other pieces of your career work, assume you will need to be competent.

2   I needed very little sleep. If I got anything close to 6 hours a night, I was in great shape with no ill effects the next day.

3   I didn't have any kids, so it was easy to come in early or work late if I needed to.

4   I worked out regularly and stayed physically fit. I attribute my ability to almost never taking a sick day to this regimen… maybe along with the fact that I didn't have any kids to bring home cooties from school :).

Out of the blue, I started to have a strange sensation of movement around me. For example, when walking down a hallway, the wall to my left would seem to move at a different speed than the wall to my right. It was very disorienting. It also sort-of felt like I was floating in one of those 3 dimensional pictures, except I already live in 3 dimensions, so it was more like 6 dimensions. It's not as cool as it sounds; as it turns out 3 dimensions are plenty.

This went on for months. During that time, I'd been to no fewer than 3 primary care doctors, 3 ENT's, 2 Neurologists, a chiropractor, allergist, had tubes in my ears, acupuncture, two brain scans, a thing called a VNG test and another test called an EMG which is basically needles pushed into every muscle in my body to see if the nerves were working correctly (they were). Then, one day I suddenly had a terrible bout of vertigo. I used to think I knew what vertigo was until I actually experienced it. It is absolutely awful and will immediately humble you. I could hear my heartbeat inside my head all the time and I discovered that it was now a struggle to walk into a dim or dark room without losing my balance. Being in the dark makes me unstable (not unstable like a disgruntled postal worker, unstable like I'm wobbly), and I also discovered stress exacerbates the issue.

So, now my high-octane outwork everyone approach (which is stressful) is no longer an option. For two months I refused to drive a car, being terrified that I would have a vertigo attack. I thought I knew what I had but not a single doctor could diagnose me. One prescribed some physical therapy, and the therapist immediately asked me if I had Meniere's disease. This is exactly what my wife and I thought it was based on all the symptoms and the research we had done. The 3rd ENT I went to was skeptical but did some tests and over time as my hearing degraded, I was formally diagnosed with Meniere's. Research indicated that there was little known about the disease or the cause, other than a very general reference to the weakening of the inner ear, and of course the cure—there isn't one. There was very limited information available. I discovered that there is a surgery that some have had success with, but based on my own personal research, only about half the surgeries were successful, and only half of the successful ones stuck (in other words, half of those opting for surgery regressed back to their original state). It is also somewhat risky, and even though I am now slowly going deaf, especially in one ear, the surgery can potentially cause deafness sooner (or so the Internet says). So, now I live in a world where I have to avoid loud noises and certain activities that could activate or trigger my vertigo. Most restaurants and all concerts are a challenge.

I find quick cuts and jumping from scene to scene on TV shows or in movies is terrible for me – many times I have to look away and ask my wife to let me know when that scene is over. There are several shows we enjoy that I now struggle to watch due to the very "jerky" way they are filmed. The company I worked for when I was first diagnosed was also pumping in "white noise" to compensate for the ridiculous open floor plan that all companies think employees like… that noise just about drove me insane. A quick digression here – I don't think I'm divulging any secret by telling you most employees don't like the open plan – in fact, they hate it – but can't say anything out of fear of being labeled as "not a team player." The open plan is a silly farce that corporations have been selling as being done "for the employee." In reality, the open plan just makes it possible to stuff more people into the same space as well as keep an eye on what everyone is doing. It's supposed to be more conducive to, and inspire collaboration, when all it really does is increase headphone sales since everyone buys a pair to block out the white noise and other distractions from everyone else in the not so quiet open space. But I digress.

Back to my health challenge… my wife was incredible—she did so much research to try to help me get better, or at least stabilized. Doctors basically didn't have any guidance, so she had to do this on her own. We tried one high-vitamin approach that ended up affecting my liver, so we had to stop that. We also discovered a low sodium diet could be helpful, so she scheduled a meeting with a dietician and started to develop an approach to feeding me low sodium meals. This was super difficult, considering there is a TON of salt in everything. Did I mention I love food… the creamier, richer, tastier the better.

This was a real shock to my system; the low sodium food was pretty bland as you would expect, and some of my favorite dishes were now untouchable. I quickly lost 15 pounds, which some people would love, but I'm a relatively small framed guy, so this was a lot of weight. The issue was I couldn't eat enough calories without going over my sodium limit. I would want more food, but I also had to keep my sodium content down. It doesn't sound like it would be hard to figure out, but it was... really hard. I also discovered that alcohol could trigger the vertigo, so I had to stop drinking alcohol. This wasn't a huge deal as I was never much of a drinker, but I did enjoy an occasional glass of wine with dinner and will admit to really liking a Guinness every now and then, and of course a good Mexican beer with my enchiladas or fajitas. All those things are now off my food and drink list. So now, not only am I "sick" I even look sick as I lost, and continued to lose, so much weight.

Fortunately, my wife is super smart and super dedicated to helping keep me healthy. She started to figure out how to cook differently, healthier, but still makes sure we have flavorful meals. We now eat much more organically and she even figured out the in-between meals snacks for me so I wasn't starving all day. With my "previous" body I could literally eat anything I wanted, all day, with no ill effects. If I ever did put on a few pounds, I would jog for a week and be back in shape... my wife often shared her dislike for my ability to do this.

I could never get enough calories to keep my weight steady—all my clothes hung off of me, and I was hungry all the time. Fortunately, after about a year, I was able to establish a consistent diet that allowed me a good breakfast, lunch and dinner with snacks in-between and even dessert at night. Although I can't gain any, my weight has stabilized, and thankfully I now have my vertigo under control. I can always "feel" an episode coming on and have some techniques to help keep it from totally debilitating me. I work hard to make sure this challenge doesn't define who I am.

I mention all of this to highlight that being "sick" didn't change the fact that I still have excellent skills and an ability to work and contribute, I just have to make sure I get better sleep, have a consistent schedule, and keep my stress in check. If and when I feel something coming on, I need to avoid triggers, which can sometimes be found in the workplace. There are a lot of very successful people diagnosed with Meniere's disease that live productive lives, and I see no reason to let it stop me from my daily life, but I've had to make some concessions. I can no longer simply "out-work" everyone – and I deliberately limit my screen time (TV, phone, computer) because it can trigger me.

Here's another not so secret reality: companies will tell you that they reasonably accommodate for someone with needs that differ from the norm and that they will not discriminate based on physical limitations (or illness). Some may, but for the most part I don't believe it, and if they do it's at the minimum required level of what they interpret as "reasonable." I had one doctor tell me NOT to put any medical issues on job submittals believing I would most certainly be excluded from any hiring process. Not sure what expertise a doctor has related to business hiring… maybe they've seen it from a worker's comp perspective, but I thought it was interesting.

It took me a while, but here's the point—you never know when something unexpected is going to happen to you. Instead of Meniere's disease, I could have been in a car accident that changed or altered my life in some way, or any other unforeseen incident or diagnosis that could impact and change a life overnight. I hope nothing ever happens to you or your family, but it is unrealistic to think nothing will and it's better to be prepared than scrambling to figure things out when it happens. I actually consider myself fortunate—I have something I can deal with, it hasn't stopped me from living a full life, and I have an incredible support system to help me when I need it. I guess the other lesson here references back to another chapter in the book… it's important to surround yourself with quality people.

As an aside—don't be afraid to challenge your doctors—they are human, too. Not only could none of them diagnose me, they didn't really try. Most of them wanted me in and out of their office as quickly as possible so they could move on to the next fully-insured paying customer.

One spoke to me like I was lying about my symptoms. Maybe people try to score prescriptions by lying or something—I'm not really sure why I was treated in such a rude and unprofessional manner. I didn't want any prescriptions, just a diagnosis. In fact, I generally don't like taking any medications; I didn't take them after several surgeries and even during a kidney stone incident, so I was definitely not looking for drugs. Suffice it to say, I fired that physician (yes, you can fire your doctor). Not a single doctor knew what I had, but a physical therapist came to the same conclusion as me, then eventually the third ENT I saw finally got it. Push others to be better, especially when it comes to your health. I literally had to "challenge" doctors to figure this out, and switch doctors until I found one dedicated enough to want to help.

Talk about potentially life changing, here's another interesting doctor story at no extra cost. I was reminded of this when I came across an old business card of a doctor I went to see a few years ago. I was having some back pain and made an appointment with a now infamous doctor. After my appointment he indicated he wanted to perform surgery on me, which, by the way, I didn't need. Something was really off about this guy, and I told my wife that there was no way he was going to touch me. This doctor acquired the nickname "Dr. Death" and is now serving life in prison… for many infractions, including crippling and killing patients due to incompetence and being under the influence during surgery.

Always listen to your inner voice—doctors are not gods, they are people, and you are allowed to challenge them. Same holds true at your job: senior leaders often attain their position because they were very good at something and earned that position and responsibility, but that doesn't mean they are infallible—you should not assume that they are all knowing and incapable of mistakes. Maybe they were really great at something, so they were put in charge of that something. History has proven that being good at the something doesn't always translate into being good at managing it. Some great players become great coaches, and some great players are terrible coaches.

Don't take your health for granted, and unless you are independently wealthy, work to save money like an over-caffeinated squirrel—you're going to need it. Also, don't stress yourself out, it can, and will take its toll on your health. While at work, contribute at a high level. When away from work, turn it off. Worrying about work doesn't change anything, but it can literally make you sick. Also, having a good partner or spouse can make life much more enjoyable, and healthier.

CHAPTER 6

Picking an Industry

HEALTHCARE, AUTOMOTIVE, MUNICIPAL, FOOD & BEVERAGE, retail, hospitality, financial, energy, travel, technology… whatever you pick, if you stay long enough, this is what the rest of your working life may look like. If, for example, you absolutely have no interest in healthcare, find a role in a different industry. Skills are transferable, but companies act like they're not, so if you don't move, be prepared to stay in that industry for a long time. My advice is to try some different things early—the more "experiences" you have in one single industry, the more likely you will be committed, or potentially stuck in that industry. There are certainly people who have made successful transitions from one industry to another, but the longer you stay with one, the harder it becomes to switch.

Picking a Specialty

Be careful when you pick an area of specialization. Let me explain.

Working in a role for a couple of years and gaining experience isn't a bad thing, but if you're not careful it can unintentionally pigeonhole your career. While you are fulfilling the duties of that first multi-year job, start to think about if it's something you want to do for the next 25-30 years. Look at the supervisors and managers above you, what they do, and what the path is to get there. Do they seem to enjoy their work, and is the work they do something you would want to do? Even if it's work you would enjoy and you think the people above you like their jobs, make sure they are respected by their peers. You don't want to work in a department or area that is viewed as the bottom of the barrel or some dumping ground of "grunt" work. Once you are in one of these areas, it can be difficult to move and other departments may view your reputation the same as the reputation of the department.

Here's something I experienced—years ago I worked in a couple of purchasing-related roles. In both cases, the areas were understaffed and seen as a servant role to other areas (more accurately subservient). I was serious about my work, I even studied to get certified in the profession, but while attending several conferences and talking to a lot of people who had been in the profession, I learned that it was going to be a difficult climb up any career growth ladder. I believe times have changed since then and purchasing and supply chain management has become a much more integral and valued part of many organizations, but at the time I knew I was at risk of being stuck in a position without any upward mobility. I was able to parlay that experience into another role that required a background of writing RFP's and evaluating lowest, best bids. I took the job and used that role to continue to take on different assignments that would provide experience outside of the purchasing path. Ironically, I later found myself working for a large Group Purchasing Organization (GPO), but it was very different than being the actual purchasing agent for an organization that didn't value the role. I'm not saying roles in the purchasing profession are not a worthy pursuit, they can certainly offer rewarding careers, but at the time (and place) I was doing it, I knew it wasn't going to provide me opportunities for growth and definitely no career path. I also knew these roles at the organizations I worked at were not perceived as important. I could have picked marketing, accounting or any number of examples at a given organization where this same situation exists—I just happened to have an example from the purchasing side.

Picking Your Spots

You shouldn't feel compelled to share every idea you have, and you don't need to have a strong opinion during every discussion, and definitely don't go running to your manager every time someone does something that annoys you. If you create a reputation for doing any of these things, when a real opportunity to shine with an idea arises, or you need to bring up a challenge with someone deviating from policy, you may simply be dismissed as the alarmist everyone has learned to ignore. Basically, what I'm saying here is pick your battles—regardless of category, not everything has the same level of importance, so really be judicious in which ones you want to champion. Build a reputation as someone who is listened to when they speak because people will know what you say is well thought out and likely meaningful.

CHAPTER 7

I Can Do More Faster... Why Do I Get Punished?

THIS TOPIC IS BECOMING LESS PROBLEMATIC AS WORKING remotely becomes more commonplace, but there are still many organizations that haven't embraced that model. Here's the scenario: you give the exact same assignment(s) to three people, two take a day and a half to do it, and one can do it in half a day. You can't offer more money or promotions to any of them, but you somehow see the person who does it quicker as a problem. Let me explain: I had an employee who could do their work faster than everyone else, and just as accurately, if not more accurate. When I would ask them to do additional work, they would ask if they did something wrong and were being punished. I said no, but identified that they had capacity, so I wanted to assign them more work. They asked why everyone else with the same title didn't get assigned double work like they did. They would also ask if there was a way to get a raise or promotion for taking on more work given their skills were better, which allowed them to do more work. I would have loved to have given either or both of these things, but it wasn't in the budget at the time, and the salary for this position wasn't super flexible (and they knew this). This was my go-to person when I needed something quick and accurate, yet I used to get frustrated with them when they didn't want to take on extra work.

I could probably argue either side of this coin, but here's where I landed: it's not their fault that the company wouldn't pay for their advanced capabilities, even though I would make the case at budget time, which, by the way, highlights the importance of making sure you work in an area that is valued. I had suggested they look for other roles, either internal or external, for something that would pay them for their advanced capabilities, but they liked the team, the work location, pay and benefits of this job. They also had some outside interests and when I would stop by their desk it was never a surprise to see their external interests up on the computer screen. I would ask if they finished such and such a project, and they would always say yes.

We had a good working relationship and would often have discussions about the optics of them "working" on outside interests while others were working on company assignments. One of their points was this: I could sit there and go slow, and no one would know any different. Instead, I get work to you early so you have more time to review, prepare, ask questions and make any necessary alterations. Their other point was if they were working remotely, I would have never known the difference. In time, I learned to really value this person. They did get me work early, the work they did was accurate and reliable, and being good wasn't a bad thing. Due to their outside interests, they weren't "hungry" to search for something more challenging, and I learned to be OK with that. The alternative was to get a slower person for the same wage that may require more supervision. No thanks. What I'm getting at is that you are going to have people who can do more than what you give them. If they are ambitious and want to grow and advance, they may let you assign them more. If this is the case, help them grow—you will find no better satisfier than watching a member of your team grow and advance professionally. There could be some who simply want to stay status quo. I do think you owe it to the person who wants to stay status quo a conversation as to why they are not advancing, and what it would take for them to do so, but don't hold someone's talent against them—they may have a good reason for staying in a role that seems to be easy for them to do.

CHPATER 8

Work Hard, Get Paid—Work Harder, Get Paid More! Maybe.

OW, YOU FOUND A PLACE THAT PAYS GOOD MONEY AND YOU discover going the extra mile pays off, literally. You deliver some really quality work, maybe do something that hasn't been done before, offer some fresh perspective... you are valued. And being valued gets you rewarded with raises, responsibility, promotions and staff. You learned that hard work gets rewarded, and that's a good thing. So, you decide to work even harder. Some may see this hard work as a way to get ahead, and it may well be... and it may even be worth it because you can make as much in one year as you used to make in three! Here's the tradeoff: if you embrace this approach, it can consume your entire life if you allow it.

Here's what else may happen: you worked so hard that you were actually doing the equivalent of two peoples' work, and when you are able to hire someone to do your old job, you discover they can only do one person's work, so now you have your new job and still retain part of your old job, too. This may require you to work after hours and on weekends to keep up.

While working 7 days a week, you find yourself sending messages and assignments regardless of what day or time it is, expecting those who receive your assignments to take action or respond. Guess what, some may work a 24/7 schedule, some may not. This is going to sound crazy to any company, but it makes perfect sense for every individual—unless something simply can't wait until regular working hours, don't do it. Even if you decide to do something after hours, don't share it or send it to your staff or colleagues until regular business hours. If you send it in the evening or on the weekend you are just going to elicit stress in the people you send it to. They may think they need to address it right away or take initiative and do the next step, which may require additional people to get involved.

You're thinking they should do it. After all, you are working on a weekend or after hours, why can't they. Here's why: after you are promoted it's likely you will be earning additional income—you may feel obliged and even happy to put in whatever hours are necessary to justify that impressive salary you are being paid. That's great, but the reality is that your staff may still be struggling to make ends meet. You have the luxury to call a plumber when a sink drips, take your car to the mechanic for a minor repair, or hire someone to mow your lawn, clean your house, or maybe pick your kids up after school. Not everyone is on equal salary footing. You may have extra time to dedicate to work because your salary provides you the aforementioned luxuries.

People on your team may need their time off to take care of a family member, or even just handle some other non-work-related responsibilities that they can't afford to pay someone else to do. The only time they have to do these things is when they are away from work. Don't mess with their free time unless it's absolutely necessary. It's awesome that you are making a great salary, but everyone may not be at the same place in life that you are, and their financial incentive to work as hard as you may not be the same.

By the way, even if every hour you work is billable and you can keep pace with the workload, it still comes at a cost… your personal life. That may mean a spouse, kids, parents, extended family, health, leisure, travel, or sleep. You may believe the salary is worth it, but there are only 24 hours in a day, and you need to allocate some of those hours for yourself. If you don't, the stress will certainly catch up with you, which can be brutal on your body & health. Stress can also be contagious and spill over onto those close to you. They don't deserve that.

Working non-stop also raises the bar and sets an expectation with your management that you will always be available. There may be situations where a specific nightly, weekly, or monthly process needs a person to manage it, or occasionally a project that requires extra attention. A good manager and a good company will find ways to schedule and rotate employees so no individual is always the one burdened with this responsibility. If rotation is not an option, good companies will provide some other means of financial or time compensation. With most jobs, there will be times you need to be available after hours or on weekends but being available every night and every weekend should not be an expectation. Some organizations have this culture, and if this expectation was made clear up front, then you shouldn't be surprised by the workload. If, however, afterhours work was sold to you as occasional and in reality, it's constant, you may need to set limits to your availability. If your boundaries are met with resistance and you prefer to have some downtime, then you may need to find a different job.

I've had a few bosses who knew I was a workhorse and would assign me more work than anyone could possibly do because they knew I would find a way to get it done. As a result, any time I tried to take time for myself or my family, I was made to feel as though I was a disappointment. If you put in 60 hours a week, they'll want 65... and why not, especially if you are an exempt employee who isn't going to earn overtime. Every extra hour you put in takes your hourly rate down. Feeling the need to be available all the time got so bad that at one point I recall being part of a conference call and was on the agenda to provide an update on some project that everyone probably hated. Anyway, I wasn't feeling well, stepped out of my office, literally ran to the restroom and urinated blood, then ran back to my office and waited to present my topic. After I was done, I messaged someone to let them know I had to step away... to the hospital. I was in terrible pain but thought I couldn't "leave my post." As it turns out, I had a kidney stone. During the trip to the hospital, I actually dialed into the call so I wouldn't miss anything. The company had a culture that made me feel compelled to stay and present my update, even though I should have been at the hospital. This should have been a clear indication to me that I was putting too much value on work and not enough on my health.

This is not to suggest you shouldn't work hard, or even put in the occasional extra hours to help out when someone is on vacation or when there is a legitimate business need, but if extra hours are needed every single day, then the team is probably understaffed and needs additional employees. I'm pretty certain if I wasn't exempt and would have received 1.5X my salary for overtime, the after-hours requests by the company would have been considerably less.

Work is part of life, but it should not BE your life. I wish I knew the formula for where the happy medium was, where you can work hard, maybe even harder than everyone else, without sacrificing your own personal well-being. For me, when I was an exempt employee, I identified what my minimum hourly rate was. Once I started to drop below that, I knew it was time to stop working for the week. I found a way to work ~50-55 hours a week (still too many if you ask current me, but far less than I had done at several points in my career). There will be occasions when large or time sensitive projects require extra time or there may be an emergency that requires extra time and commitment; this happens and you can't leave the rest of the team or the company hanging—and I'm not suggesting you should—but the years will pass quickly, and you'll look back and wonder why you thought putting in 11-12 hour days every day was necessary.

There are some roles that offer incredible rewards for being "on" 24/7 (huge salaries, stock options or grants, and bonuses) and the time these people dedicate to work may set them up for life financially. If you have one of these roles or can realistically advance to one, it may be worth the time investment... at least for a while. If you are not one of those people, working non-stop will just wear you out and you may find yourself regretting it later. Just remember, there needs to be a balance—keep some part of your life separate from work. I've worked for some bad companies and some great companies, and what I can assure you is when either version decides you are no longer worth the investment, they will not think back to all the missed personal time you sacrificed for the greater good of the company, they will simply cut you loose and move on. They really will. You should always do your best, give your best and be a good contributor, leader and teammate, but remember, work is just part of your life, not the whole thing.

CHAPTER 9

Everyone Likes Me... Well, Almost Everyone

FOR WHATEVER REASON, THERE WILL BE PEOPLE WHO JUST DON'T like you... and the feeling may be mutual. It may be jealousy, fear, some inappropriate bias based on race, gender, political affiliation, religion, or maybe you just look like someone they once knew and didn't like. Maybe you made a bad first impression and they will never give you another chance, or perhaps you have resources they need, said no to one of their projects, or are just in their way (i.e. they want your job). I've even seen a dislike for people from one company toward another when a merger or acquisition occurs. The reason doesn't matter, but what does matter is how you deal with them. I've handled this a few different ways... here are a couple of things I would not recommend.

1 Don't try to prove them wrong by going out of your way to be helpful and friendly, showing them how great you are.

2 Don't be the exact same back to them; if they are mean, passive aggressive or rude you don't need to return the favor.

For the first one, don't spend extra energy trying to prove to someone who has unfairly judged you that they are wrong. You probably have enough going on at work and in your life, so why should you spend any energy or effort on a person who, for whatever reason, has already pre judged you. In the second example, it's also not worth your time to treat them the same way. All this does is reinforce their already biased opinion of you, and if others see you acting this way, it may impact their assessment of you.

My suggestion—take the high road. Continue to do good work, be nice, be professional and expect the same from others. Don't sink to their level or you may get stuck down there or become permanently tagged as a problem. Also, don't make it a personal thing or whine to your manager; it's not grade school and you should be able to handle your own problems... not to mention, if you go to your manager, you just made your problem their problem, which is likely one more problem than they need. When you do go to your manager with an issue, make sure it's a real issue, not something petty.

Here's the reality: not everyone is going to like everyone else. If there is someone who doesn't like you or you don't like them, it doesn't mean you can't work together effectively... deliver good work, and maybe over time establish a level of respect and trust, just skip having coffee or lunch with them. If it doesn't work out, at least you know you did your part to try.

I remember a couple of people who were especially challenging for me over the years... really, I think there were only 2, which isn't bad given I've been working since I was a teenager. Anyway, these individuals would do whatever they could to create headwind for me or be hurdles to either me or my team. I learned to keep cool and continue to focus on my own game and the things I could control. One eventually became a good teammate who I established a working relationship with. I did that by consistently being helpful, supportive and showed a sincere openness to wanting to help them succeed. Basically, I won them over by being a good teammate. The other never came around and for whatever reason simply did not approve of me being alive. Nothing I can do about that other than do good work and continue to establish and build on my positive reputation with others. I didn't allow it to become an issue for me, but if they want it to be an issue for them, that's their prerogative.

OK, I know I said that only 2 people really disliked me over my long working career – that is simply naïve thinking. These were 2 that I knew about, the reality is there were likely many more. The actual number may have been 20 or 50. The other reality is if a person who doesn't like you is also the same person who can fire you, that one person is all it takes. The truth is you never really know what's in someone's heart or what they are thinking, but as I am reminded on a daily basis – some people can be awesome and some people just suck, so protect yourself. The easiest way to do that is to consistently contribute by producing quality, defendable work.

I know I'm making it sound like you should be paranoid and that everyone is out to get you. That is not the case at all; in fact, the examples of challenging people I described are more exception than rule, but they can also be the ones who consume a disproportionate amount of your energy if you let them.

CHAPTER 10

If You Are Good, Hire People Just Like You

THERE WILL BE TIMES WHEN YOU "INHERIT" STAFF, AND OTHER times when you get to pick your own. When inherited, there isn't much you can do other than hope they are talented and do your best to continue to develop them to be their best. My approach is to always make any staff member more knowledgeable and marketable, either for internal or external roles. I found if I took care of people and let them know I had their best interest in mind, they would do their part to take care of me, and of course, the company. When I first started hiring staff, I looked for traits that were similar to mine—I knew I was good at what I did and was successful, so I was basically the blueprint for who to hire. This worked… for a little while. It makes life easy at first; you speak the same language and seem to be in synch with projects, assignments and your general approach to work. Over time, however, you start to realize you need additional perspective.

You'll find yourself in meetings where colleagues will ask a question about your work and identify areas you've overlooked or simply got wrong. This happens when the entire team thinks and works the same way. It is really important to have a broad spectrum of backgrounds on any team, as it can create a much more effective approach to solving business problems. There are likely exceptions where it may make sense to have very similar skill sets and experiences working together, but looking back at my career, I know the best teams I was part of always had representation from many different backgrounds. In today's terms, this is known as inclusion and diversity. I am a huge supporter of this philosophy, not because the company has some box they need to check off showing they don't discriminate, but because diverse teams make for a better work product, and when people feel included, they will contribute more often and more effectively. When looking for a candidate to fill an open position, a lot of times you may ask the broader team if they know of anyone. This is great; the recommended resource is a known entity and is obviously good enough to be recommended by a team member. The downside is that this candidate may be exactly like the person recommending them. Then, when you have another opening, you may have these two staff members recommending another candidate who is exactly like them, again. You need to be careful you don't fill your team with all the same person—I promise you; different perspectives will make the team better.

I was fortunate to work on many talented and capable teams and looking back I know those teams were special because they were comprised of people with a variety of backgrounds and skills. Not everyone always loved one another, but the variety is part of what made us good— and at times really good or even great. I remember at times being frustrated by someone only to go back to my desk and think, wow, they were right, and I hadn't even considered that. This is valuable.

One special team I was part of had people who were younger, older, athletic, homebodies, had kids, didn't have kids, were cat people, were dog people, single, divorced, married, introverts, extroverts and came from different gender and cultural backgrounds. They all took their jobs seriously and wanted to contribute to the betterment of the team. The work we did was dynamic and interesting, which definitely helped. A level of respect permeated throughout, and there was an opportunity for everyone to contribute. There were some bumps here and there: some people left, some people joined—which can change the dynamic—but in general, it was a highly effective team. Like many managers, I removed roadblocks and did my best to deflect distractions, but basically, my role was to assure we had the right ingredients for a good group, to provide clear expectations, direction, guidance and opportunity, then just act as the straw that stirred the drink.

I believe the hardest part of managing a high performing team is the inability to promote or reward everyone who deserves it, as a company usually has some limitations on this front. When promotions or salary increases aren't in the cards, you can still provide different types of incentives to generate team satisfaction… including interesting work, broader exposure outside of their direct area of expertise, educational and certification opportunities, chances to present to colleagues & leadership, ability to attend interesting seminars or conferences, and opportunities to lead projects & teams. My philosophy was to make sure the team members were as marketable as possible for internal opportunities or, if there was no clear career path for them, provide them with the experience and skills they would need to find an external growth opportunity. I didn't want to lose anyone, but I didn't want to hold anyone back, either.

The takeaway here is to make sure you either build a team or are part of a team that has many different perspectives, as it's those differences that makes each individual and the team valuable. Don't be afraid of someone who doesn't literally or figuratively look like you; I discovered some of the highest quality people when I became more open to embracing differences. The teams I worked on were better for having variety and I believe being part of those teams helped me grow professionally and personally. Additionally, it's also possible to get creative in how to keep people motivated and happy even when financial incentives are not readily available. If people really like what they do, like the environment they do it in, and know you are looking out for their best interests, you will have the ingredients for a high performing team.

That Person Is a Tool!

If you have a team to manage, be sure to use them correctly. Think of them as individual tools in a toolbox. You have a level, a couple of screw-drivers, wrenches, stud finder, tape measure, hammer, duct tape (duct tape isn't always the best solution, but in a pinch it can be used to solve problems in a variety of ways). If you are hanging a picture, depending on your approach you will likely need the stud finder, level, tape measure and hammer. You can try to use the "tap on the wall" approach to finding a stud, but may end up with multiple holes in the wall before you actually find it. You can try to use the tape measure instead of a level, but you will probably end up with a crooked picture. Using a wrench to tap in a nail instead of a hammer may work, but it's going to be less than optimal and will probably leave some bruised and smashed fingers. The point here is this: use your people the correct way and don't be upset when you assign a wrench job to a hammer person and they fail. This also underlines the importance of having a diverse set of skills on the team... 6 hammers aren't always needed. It also never hurts to have a roll of duct tape around—in fact, I would definitely have one of them around. There are other ways to hang a picture, of course—this is just an example—no need to send me notes about using a laser level or some better method.

CHAPTER 11

Choose How to Respond

FOR A TIME IN MY CAREER I WOULD RESPOND TO PEOPLE AS IF I were a mirror. What I mean by that is that I tended to treat people the way they treated me; I literally mirrored back what I received.

I received an email from a colleague who was less than polite in their message to me. I responded professionally, but also with a similar tone. This person then called me out for having a blustery tone with them. I explained that I was simply responding with the same tone I received. I suggested they check with someone they trust; have them read both messages without any narrative about the situation and get their take. To my surprise, they did, and even more surprising, they apologized to me.

I didn't always reply this way, but this email really rubbed me the wrong way. It was likely a cumulative thing given I had received other similarly toned emails from this person, who I believe felt entitled to act however they wanted considering their fancy title. What I wanted to achieve in this example was to let this person, who was known for being less than subtle in emails, know that their tone and words had consequences. I was in a leadership role at the time and was pretty well thought of by my manager, so I felt I had some latitude to help improve this person's correspondence style. This may sound manipulative, but they were using their position as a way to try to intimidate other people, maybe unintentionally, but still. I was at the same level and was not intimidated and saw an opportunity to correct some poor behavior. I also followed up in person to make sure we were OK—they appreciated this. They also asked if I really interpreted their messages as negative. I was honest, and added that it didn't matter if I was OK with it because I had regular interactions with them and could address any concerns in person, but challenged them to think about how a lower titled person with little interaction with them might interpret a message like this. We debated the need to be touchy feely in an email a little, but in the end, I think they understood that it could be difficult to receive an email like this and acknowledged that it could also potentially damage their reputation. The people who received terse messages would talk and that talk would then bubble up to their managers, and so on. I saw a concerted change in their writing style after this "incident." Good for them for being open to feedback and to show a willingness to change. After a while, I realized it wasn't my job to save the world from every bully and I picked my battles instead of mirroring everyone I dealt with. Instead, I just stayed consistent with my own approach.

More managerial stuff… Thinking back to when I was a young, new manager, I thought I had to show a level of toughness and have the courage to reprimand someone if needed. What I learned instead was that being respected is much more impactful than being tough. If I would talk to someone about a mistake or a developmental opportunity and I did it in a way that they knew it would help them, it was a much easier conversation, and typically had a better outcome. Just yelling at someone isn't very effective; at least, not that I've seen. People prefer dealing with someone who is nice. Even if the feedback is corrective in nature, the way the message is delivered can make all the difference. If you are on the receiving end of being yelled at by a supervisor, try to steer them in the direction of turning it into a learning opportunity. If they are good, they should be receptive to this… but now you have a responsibility to show that you have learned and will not make the same mistake again.

Being nice doesn't mean you have to be a pushover. I've done that and I've learned: once a pushover, always a pushover. Letting someone continually get away with either breaking the rules or creating their own rules makes others lose confidence and maybe even respect for you. You can't allow some people to have a different rule book than others—and you have to follow the same rules, too.

Being consistent also helps build credibility, and people will know what to expect from you, instead of wondering if they are getting Dr. Jekyll or Mr. Hyde. If you change your mind all the time or jump between management styles you will generate a lot of eye rolls and will not be taken seriously. It's definitely easier to go "by the book" early on, and occasionally loosen the reins than to say yes to every exception and expect anyone to take you seriously when you try to hold them accountable.

CHAPTER 12

SPEAK UP!

WHEN GIVEN AN OPPORTUNITY TO SPEAK UP... SPEAK UP. I USED to follow the rule of only adding new and pertinent information to a conversation. I would add to a discussion if something was left out, otherwise I would stay quiet. People that knew me understood my approach—no need for superfluous conversation. They knew that when I spoke it was going to be something that I thought was either missed or was additive to the conversation. Those who didn't know me just saw me as a church mouse who was timid and didn't want to engage—on at least one occasion, this cost me a growth opportunity.

I knew several colleagues who would speak just to be heard. Their approach was to just agree with what someone else had said. I found this silly, but others saw them as involved in the dialogue and "contributing" to the conversation. I saw them as parrots, but it seemed to work. Instead of adding to the conversation, they would ask someone to clarify what they meant, maybe occasionally adding value by getting a deeper understanding of an opinion, but usually it was just a way to be seen and heard without having to have a strong opinion about anything.

Good leaders will see through this, but don't assume you will always report to good leaders. Over time, I learned to speak up more, even if just to say "I agree with what has been said, I particularly agree with point such and such..." Some of the companies I worked at wanted to hear people talk, so I talked. Not all companies will be like this, but you can usually determine pretty quickly if they are and adjust your approach as needed. This doesn't mean you should say something just to be provocative, rather pick your spots and/or if you do have a strong opinion on something, share it. Depending on the organization you will get a sense for where the line is.

Also, if you are in a meeting, at a conference, or on a call and you are thinking something based on what you are hearing, don't be afraid to express what you are thinking. Definitely feel out the room first, obviously; don't blurt out something in a tense situation, but if appropriate, express yourself. I can't tell you how many times in my career I thought something during a session that I kept to myself only to have someone else say the exact thought I was having and being celebrated for sharing it. Make sure what you want to share is relevant, but don't be shy… unless you are in a culture that doesn't really want to hear others' ideas. If that is the culture, and you really need your job, just agree with what is being said and go along to get along (as long as it's ethically OK to do so) until you can find something that better fits your values.

Depending on your position, there may be times when people want to hear from you so they know where you stand on a topic; they literally may want to take their cues from you. If you have achieved the status of influencer and your opinion is important to a larger group, it probably makes sense to speak up, but also be aware that your words matter, so choose them wisely.

Another time to speak up is to say please and thank you. Like being nice, saying these two things is free and could generate a significant ROI for you. Everyone wants a good performance review, and everyone wants more money, but I would also tell you people really want to be recognized for their work, and to be thanked for a job well done. When doing this, it needs to be sincere, or it won't have any impact. In fact, if it's not sincere it may have the opposite impact than you were hoping for. You will build significant good will by thanking people for their efforts. We all know that a company pays you to work, and some people think please and thank you are unnecessary, after all "it's their job." Wrong—it is extremely necessary. Using these phrases can also be contagious which is awesome and can breed an appreciative culture. When people know they are going to be asked to do something in a polite way, and be thanked for doing it, life becomes much simpler. There is no cost to do this, but the payoff can be significant. Thank you.

In addition to please and thank you, another act that should be carried out is the actual in person acknowledgment of appreciation. By default, please and thank you already indirectly indicate appreciation, but when someone does something that goes above and beyond or does something they didn't have to do, but did anyway, or in general makes your life easier, better, or less stressful, it's OK to take a minute and literally let them know you appreciate them. I'm not talking about an IM or text saying thanks—that's definitely nice, but if this person really helps make your day on a regular basis, take a minute to let them know in person.

I once helped a relatively new employee in a different department learn some semi-complex processes. I knew that once the processes could be understood, understanding the business would be easy for them. I was a little selfish as I knew if they were good at their job, the interactions we would have with their department (and them) would be better, too. I spent a lot of time walking them through details and made myself available for calls and even helped review their work when requested. I did this because they needed help, but they also made it easy to do. They acknowledged my effort, thanked me for it, told me they appreciated me and even shared their appreciation on calls or in group meetings. I established a good working relationship with this person, and they were always willing to pitch in to help if I ever needed it. I had the pleasure of watching them grow and advance, and even years later they still thanked me for helping them get their feet under them early on. Any time someone would tell me how much they appreciated me, I would play it cool and say something like thanks, no problem, but this kind of personal acknowledgement always stuck with me.

All my good managers and leaders showed a level of appreciation, the not so good ones usually didn't. The lousy managers still got 100% from me, as I was paid to do a job, but the good ones always got 110% plus, and a willingness to go above and beyond any time they needed it. Don't just compliment someone thinking you can "play them" and get more work out of them; but if someone has earned a compliment, pay it to them. This goes for people in your home life, too.

If someone compliments you and you know they sincerely appreciate what you do, I'm guessing you'll feel like any effort expended was worth it, and you might even do more for them. It's always easier working somewhere your talents are appreciated. OK, group hug!

CHAPTER 13

Sometimes You Have to Eat a Crap Sandwich...

EVEN IF YOU WORK AT A TERRIFIC COMPANY, THERE ARE GOING TO be times you will have to deal with difficult situations, difficult people and unforeseen circumstances that can make your work life feel less than ideal. Get used to it; that's how life works. Although it would be nice, you simply can't control every variable. Here are some things that may happen:

- A senior level executive who always forgets your name, reminding you just how unimportant you are.

- Someone else getting the promotion or choice assignment you wanted.

- A less than ideal seating / desk location right next to the elevators or bathroom.

- A trip or conference you wanted to attend but weren't invited to.

- A manager that plays favorites... when you're not the favorite.

- A prevalence of do as I say, not as I do from leadership.

- Having a workspace next to the person who brings tuna every day for lunch... and eats at their desk.

+ Preparing for a presentation only to have your time cut.

+ The company changes policy related to something you were finally eligible for.

+ Not getting a desired promotion, raise or bonus.

+ Having to work the night or weekend shift when you don't want to.

+ Being assigned to a new team or manager where you become the lowest on the totem pole.

Whatever the specific scenario, you are going to be faced with some of these and many other crap sandwiches throughout your career. Sometimes, you just have to choke a few bites down and move on; corporate life isn't fair and you're not the only one who gets served this meal. Everyone is going to face some level of adversity at some point—do your best to handle it with as much dignity and class as possible and make sure you learn from the situation. For example, if you had a terrible desk location near the bathrooms, next time your team moves or another desk becomes available you should speak up and ask for a better location. Definitely pick your battles—you don't want a reputation as a complainer, but knowing everyone's bowel elimination routines because you sit next to a bathroom is not a transferrable skill that is going to make you more marketable and is probably a battle worth picking - at least it would be for me.

If the only item on the menu is a crap sandwich or if it's the only item you ever get fed, you may want to look for a different path. It's one thing to have to take an occasional bite, but you should not have to eat a full one daily. There are plenty of other places to work that have a better menu selection.

Some places just can't help themselves and people get accustomed to what they are fed believing that there is no alternative. This is not the case: if you are miserable, you have the power to change that. Life is too short to be told to eat lousy food every day. You may feel a sense of loyalty to the company for providing you a job, but you should always have a greater sense of loyalty to yourself. Remember, no one is going to look out for you like you will. You are allowed to have an expectation of being treated fairly and professionally, and if you are not, it may be time to find a place that will. Change can be difficult and scary, but life is short, and you shouldn't spend a third of it somewhere that makes you unhappy.

CHAPTER 14

Would You Like to Step Outside?

You know what you are doing. Your boss knows what they are doing. The people on your team know what they are doing, and finally a manager or other leadership position opens up and it's an opportunity for everyone to move up one spot. Instead, the company decides to bring in someone from the outside. If there truly isn't a good internal option, this may make perfect sense. However, when you know there are several internal candidates that can do the job, an external hire can be perplexing, especially when it could show the rest of the team that there is opportunity to grow and advance. There are many reasons this can happen—here are a few:

- The department may not be well thought of and management thinks they need to change things up.

- No one in the department has a good relationship with management and therefore management has no idea of the talent that is available.

- In order to move forward, the area needs a fresh perspective or a level of expertise that is missing internally.

- The person being brought in is a friend or acquaintance of someone more senior in the organization and they are filling the role with a friend.

There are many other reasons, but regardless of why an external person is brought in, it can be a real demotivator for everyone.

Here's the quick lesson—if things aren't moving for you, you may want to consider being that exciting new external hire somewhere else. There is definitely risk in this, but it can also help elevate your career more quickly than you might be able to do at your current company. I know this can be hard, especially if you are in a tight labor market. Weigh the various options and make an educated decision. By the way, external hires typically get a better salary than someone promoted from within, so if you move around strategically, you may be able to accelerate your salary more quickly, too. Small incremental annual raises are nice, but usually only keep you even with inflation—promotions are almost always more financially rewarding.

Unless contractually obligated to do so, you don't have to tell anyone that you are looking. If you do take an outside role, make sure it's one that you know you can do—this doesn't guarantee success, as there are a lot of factors in play, so definitely exercise some caution when doing this. For example, don't jump from director to VP somewhere chasing a great title and increased pay if you think you are going to fall on your face and fail. It's OK to be challenged by the role, but not overwhelmed. At the same time, don't overthink it.

By the way, the more time you have, the more risk you can take. It's kind of like the stock market; if you are relatively young, it's easier to recover from a potential mistake. You can, and should, take greater risks when the time horizon is long.

If things are looking up for you and there are opportunities to grow and get raises and promotions where you are, there may not be any urgency—but you should still keep active and engaged with your network; you never know when something will change. If you are continually passed over for opportunities that you truly believe you are qualified to do and should have been considered for, then you may need to start thinking about other options.

One final thought… if an external hire is brought in and you decide to stay, do your best to be a good team player. If you are anything but helpful, management may feel the need to replace you. They may also have someone who they want to bring in, and you don't want to give them a reason to do this. Keep in mind, not all outside hires work out, so if they don't work and you've been a helpful and productive contributor, when they leave, you may still have your chance to advance.

Getting out of line may be another option—I remember my wife and I visiting a large theme park in the Southeastern United States and there was a much promoted new roller coaster everyone wanted to ride—we did too, so we got in line to ride it (for the record, I actually get somewhat sick on roller coasters, so I stand in line with her, and she rides it). The line we were in was long, very long and although the ride itself may have been worth a reasonable wait, we decided there were at least five other roller coasters and even more non roller coaster rides that we could be taking advantage of instead of passively waiting for this one. We went from being number 2,345 in line to number 4, then rode it again, then moved on to another ride, and another. Sometimes if things look like they are going to take forever to happen, you may need to make a move. By getting out of line, we were still able to have a great time, and even made more of our day than we would have if we had waited. The career correlation is obvious—don't ever believe there is only one option for you. If you look around, sometimes even close by, you may discover many other opportunities that will provide you with the same experience you desire, without the long wait.

CHAPTER 15

Honey & Carrots

YOU MAY HAVE HEARD THE SAYING THAT YOU CATCH MORE FLIES with honey than vinegar. Put aside any debates about why you would want to catch flies and accept the concept that you can attract more people with sweetness. I generally agree with this, and when possible, I try to be respectful, supportive and positive… and of course, nice. I believe in the philosophy that being nice doesn't cost anything, and at the end of the day you can go through life engaging with people in a positive way or being a jerk, which will do little more than bring out the worst in others. Your paycheck is going to be the same either way, but why go through life being the person everyone else tries to avoid.

To keep it simple, defaulting to being nice is a usually better than the alternative. This doesn't mean being fake nice, then going behind someone's back and talking badly about them or undermining their efforts. Be nice, but also be professional. Being nice doesn't mean you have to cave to people—you can disagree with someone or even be politely tough with someone. You can take an opposing position without resorting to name-calling or rude behavior. Here's the other great thing about being nice: when you do have to be tough, it really carries some weight. People will think "dang, so and so never gets upset, this must be serious". Just be sure to pick your spots when doing this.

I used to believe it was always easier to start out "tough"; my thought was that it's easier to start tough and be nice when necessary, rather than starting nice and having to switch to tough. But, years of experience has taught me different. Being nice doesn't mean you don't have to make tough decisions; it's more about how you approach those decisions and how you treat others in the process.

Enough about honey; let's talk about carrots. Another famous saying is about using a carrot instead of a stick—it has to do with reward and punishment, and there is some research that suggests it doesn't work… but I needed something to go with the honey example, so roll with it.

I have a real-world example… I was at a company that implemented a new CRM system and we needed to get the sales reps trained and utilizing the tool. The idea was exactly what CRM promises: having a system of record, standardized sales process, better insight to your pipeline, assigning leads via marketing campaigns, having data to identify sales cycles, ability to forecast, simplified & insightful reporting, knowledge of what products each customer had purchased, participation in company programs, the customer risk level, segmentation, collaboration tools, customer contact information, and a hundred other fields and attributes. Prior to the system, it was basically 100 people calling each other and passing multiple spreadsheets around trying to put together a pipeline and forecast with everything else I mentioned, handled as disparate standalone processes. A real nightmare. Well, as is the case at many companies, change is difficult and can be met with resistance. Telling the sales team that they were going to input all their contacts, leads and opportunities and keep them updated wasn't exactly the great news they had all been waiting to hear. If you work in an organization that can mandate adoption, great. If you don't, you may need to get creative in how you get things done.

I remember all the reps flying in to do a training session on the new platform. We rented an offsite training facility near the corporate office large enough to accommodate the entire team, put together a curriculum and rotated users through the various sessions. We kept it light, engaging, and I think fun (as much fun as learning data input can be) and made them feel important. Honestly, they were important to the company and to the adoption of the new system. During the training session, one of the top sales reps sat at a computer at the back of the room with their feet up on the desk and read the paper. Seriously. This person had great relationships with their clients and there was no way the company was going to remove them from their accounts. They had no incentive to use the system, and although leadership could talk to them, it wasn't going to have much impact. And where did they find a newspaper, I didn't know they still existed... my guess is they picked it up at the airport or hotel on the way in, but this isn't about the newspaper.

Back to the CRM system... when a deal was sold, the sales rep would enter it for the first time in the new system as it (the deal) was closed, then would pick up their commission. There was no tracking of the opportunity through the pipeline, no forecast, no idea how long the sale took, no sharing of best practices, etc. Here comes the carrot: we enhanced the sales process to include required stages throughout that would trigger certain activities, and eventually release the commission. In other words, if the deal wasn't tracked in the system, they wouldn't get paid. It was hard to change behavior, as the system was seen as big brother looking over their shoulder instead of a tool to help them be more efficient and effective. In the end, the tool became more widely adopted, and there was less animosity toward it. We tried some other carrot-like things to get even deeper engagement. For example, collaborating with each other within the tool... but the incentive we used to entice them wasn't substantial enough or meaningful to the users. If you plan to use this approach, make sure whoever you are working with likes carrots, or at least the type of carrots you are using as incentive. Incentives have to be meaningful, or they're not really incentives at all.

CHAPTER 16

Different Kinds of Employees & Co-Workers

THERE ARE ALL KINDS OF PEOPLE AND PERSONALITIES WHICH CAN definitely make work productive and even enjoyable, but this variety can also create challenges. Below are some of the different categories of people you might encounter—there are many more, but these are a few I've experienced over the years.

The Consumer—These are people who take and take... and take. If someone only takes from you, with no offsetting contribution, you are being used. They will take your time, knowledge, contacts, credit for your work, you name it, they'll take it—all to try to look good or advance their career. They don't care if it comes at your expense as long as it helps their cause. If you continue to allow them to consume you, it will drain you of everything until you have nothing left to give. If someone is doing this to you, stop the cycle. Set expectations that you require some form of "give" to offset their corresponding take. If they are unwilling to comply, then you should turn off the faucet and let them look for someone else to consume.

The Instigator—These are the people who provoke others into action but never put their own necks on the line. They will talk big behind closed doors and goad others into action that may be controversial or even career damaging. They will occasionally speak up, but only when they know their opinion is already the prevailing thought. Don't get pulled into their web of negativity, even when what they are saying may have a thread of truth. Their perspective may have some value, but it is only a single perspective. Take what you can and use it as one input to your decision-making process. Their insight or opinion should definitely not be your only input.

The Confident and Entitled—These people may think they don't have to prove themselves, but rather some combination of background credentials alone should be enough to justify promotions or appointments to management and leadership positions. The other trait they may possess is an excessive amount of confidence. Real confidence comes when you've prepared for something and know you can execute and deliver, which is not the same as just being "confident" in general. I've experienced many people full of hollow confidence, with no clue how to actually do anything. Sadly, I've also seen some leaders judge people on hollow confidence instead of based on actual capability. These overly confident people may even get inserted into positions ahead of others based on their ability to talk a good game about their confidence instead of any real competency. I really wish I was making this up.

Some traits of people who possess actual confidence may include the ability to learn and grasp concepts quickly, and consistently deliver on defined goals. Hollow confidence is something that was learned through receiving too many participation trophies, thinking that simply showing up means they are entitled to opportunity and rewards. The fake it 'til you make it approach, which I am not a big fan of, is also common for those with hollow confidence. Can you imagine choosing your surgeon based on this type of confidence!?

These individuals may also be inclined to enlist your time to "teach" them, so they no longer have to fake it. I always think it's OK to teach someone who wants to learn, but don't become the personal tutor for these people. They will siphon everything you have and toss you aside when there is no more knowledge to absorb. If you work in an environment that rewards "confidence," you may want to start acting more confident—I can only assume there are plenty of articles and books on the topic. If you really want to continue to make yourself more marketable, I would suggest focusing on competence first, which will fill you with solid & legitimate confidence related to your vocation.

The Fact Giver—A fact giver always feels compelled to tell you something regardless if they actually know anything. Let's say you are traveling down a road and it comes to a T in the road and the only two choices are left or right. If you ask a fact giver which way to go, and they don't know the answer, they will factually tell you "not straight." True and accurate, but not terribly helpful. When a fact giver knows an answer, they can be tremendously helpful but know both when to ask and not ask them questions. If you are looking for an opinion, it may be hard to pull one out of them; they prefer to live in a world of stating truths and may not be great with abstract thinking. This is not necessarily a negative thing; it's just how they are wired.

The Overly Nice—These people start every conversation with a compliment and are sugary sweet. The ones who act this way to overcompensate for a skill set shortcoming can be a challenge. It's hard to be mad at these people, even when they don't deliver as expected, and although it's great having someone around that is full of compliments, the work has to get done. The hard truth is, nice is only part of the success equation, and with everything being equal I prefer nice over mean any day. However, if they are not contributing in a way that is expected or required, you are going to have to deal with them. Eventually others will have to pick up their workload or the team will start to miss deliverables, which can generate friction, bad feelings and even erode morale. Nice is good, but competence is a must have component. It may seem like a double standard because unlike nice people, sometimes you have to coach mean people not to be mean, but whether mean or nice, people still need to be competent.

The Independent—Some employees are good and decide that they no longer need guidance and will just do what they think is important vs. what they are asked or assigned to do. They don't care that you may have additional clarifying information that determined a specific course of action; rather, they have their own ideas on what is important to the company (as long as it's also important to them). These people can be maddening. On one hand, they can be very smart and talented, but deviating from what has been clear directional guidance can make you look bad more than them—let me explain.

When one of these people do what they want instead of what you need, it looks like you didn't know how to explain the need, don't have control of your staff, or don't know how to lead. With these types, my advice is to nip it in the bud early. They may question why they have to do something, which can be a fair question, but sometimes they just need to do what is assigned. I wouldn't suggest saying "because I told you to," rather let them know there is a need and although they were not part of the conversation it doesn't mean it's not legitimate. Some of these people also don't want to take direction from you because they think they are smarter and want to talk directly to the requestor, especially when it's a higher titled person. Be careful with this—there are times it may make sense, and I'm never against empowering people, but I have found that some people go over your head to try to impress your boss or other higher titled individuals for less than sincere reasons.

There may be times having a person talk directly to the requestor makes perfect sense, but if you are the manager, this is your decision, not theirs. There may be good reason the work is going through a manager first, and questioning you just adds potential and unnecessary complications to the work. I managed some teams whose skills were in high demand and people would seek them out because they needed those skills for their personal projects. As the manager, I had to protect the team from taking on work that would consume their time and potentially make them miss other commitments. They may have thought it was exciting to be in demand, and it may have even made them feel important to do side projects, but being diverted from other assignments could impact a lot of other people.

If you have a good boss, you can let them in on the desired approach and work together to provide clear expectations around hierarchical boundaries. If you work in a nurturing culture, there may already be development programs in place that can be leveraged to help provide a path for these people. If you work in a cut-throat culture, protect yourself as they will learn that going over your head or around you may be rewarded. I've also seen a tendency for these folks to believe it benefits them when someone else looks bad, believing it makes them look good. The basic lesson here is don't let them push you around; address issues early and protect yourself as they are definitely looking out for themselves.

The Force of Nature—Speaking of people who only think of themselves, there are some that truly believe they are smarter than most… and want everyone else out of their way. Similar to the Independent described in the previous paragraph, but much bolder. They will literally question you in front of others, limit sharing information to try to make you look uninformed while making themselves look knowledgeable and will only give full & complete updates when decision makers are present to witness their impressive intellect in person. They are open to doing things only one way—theirs—and will do everything in their power to mold things into the shape they want.

People like this are difficult to manage, can be passive aggressive and will create tremendous headwind for you. These are not the "give them an inch, they take a mile" people; they are "give them an inch they take 6 miles." I find a direct conversation with these types is important but be aware the conversation will likely be met defensively, and they will try to pin any issues on you, not them. If you have a good boss, you may also want to give them a heads up about the situation so they are not caught off guard and they can watch for detrimental behavioral patterns. More often than not, good leaders see through this, but as I like to say, not everyone is a good leader. Headwind is not good in a work environment;

it is inefficient and devours the fuel and energy of everyone it touches. Act quickly to correct inappropriate behavior and if it can't be fixed, help them find a different role that will embrace and reward their ambition. If you are a Force of Nature, make sure you work somewhere that welcomes the extremely ambitious type and has a competitive culture for you to flourish in.

The Demanding Leader—Do you have a manager or leader who seems to be really demanding, maybe even intense in their demeanor and approach to work? They may act this way because they are trying to achieve certain goals that will unlock personal financial incentives. Their incentive and compensation package may include stock and / or bonuses that are more than what you make in a year… maybe a lot more. Money can alter some people and turn them into something unrecognizable once they get a taste of it. They want paid, and you are a tool to help them achieve that goal; this is reality. Remember, good leaders can lead without being mean, demeaning, angry or unrealistic in their expectations of you… but not everyone is a good leader. You just need to understand their motivation.

Do your best to work with them, be helpful, and if you are willing to make those same time sacrifices you may even be able to grow into a role that is eligible for those big bonuses, too. Just don't lose your identity or become someone you're not out of a desire to advance or chase money. It's hard; we all know money can make things better and can literally buy financial security for your future. It can also make you do funny things like ignore family, ignore your health, never take time off or vacations, and potentially become someone you're not. Money is definitely important, but so is your health, family, ethics and dignity.

The Bus Driver—The Wheels on the Bus Go Round and Round… Do not be surprised if someone throws you under the proverbial bus. People can be awesome but people can also suck. The ones who suck may need to deflect blame to try to cover up their own deficiencies or incompetence to make you look bad so they or someone else can look good; it's their modus operandi—or perhaps they are just sadistic. Build up a good reputation as someone who is competent, consistently delivers quality work and is accountable for their output. You can always use some good will deposits for when you do make a legitimate mistake; as all humans do. The bus thrower underer's (if that is even a term) will pounce when you make a mistake, and you need to be prepared to weather that storm. Also, protect and defend yourself, especially if you have been wrongly accused of something. You should take responsibility for your actions and mistakes but you are not required to take on the responsibilities for others actions or mistakes. The opposite of this is also true, i.e. don't steal credit. If someone steals yours, make sure you address this with them. Give them an opportunity to set the record straight, and if they don't, it's fair for you to set it straight. Do it in a professional way, but work is hard, and you deserve credit for your efforts.

Stories From the Bus Stop—I once had someone who insisted I attend a meeting 10 minutes before it started, then proceeded with a presentation that impacted my area of responsibility, which of course I had not seen prior to the meeting. They were trying to make me look bad in front of a large group including some executive leaders in the meeting—more accurately, they were trying to make themselves look good by making me look bad. I was able to handle myself fine, as I knew my area well and could talk to all the points being made, but when asked what I thought of the presentation, I suggested I would have to review it and give it some additional thought, but would report back. This was enough to tell everyone I hadn't seen the work. To my surprise, one of the executives asked the person presenting if they received input from me or anyone on my team… the answer was no, and the implication was clear. This made them dislike me even more, but I wasn't going to allow them to throw me, or my team, under a bus. For the record, I don't know what I ever did to attract this level of dislike—it really was weird—and for a little while it bothered me until I considered the source and remembered that 99 out of 100 people had a different opinion of me.

In another example, I had someone say things that were complete lies about the team I was working on, and indirectly about me. I had to decide how to handle it, so I defended the team and myself.... strongly. I'm glad I did, as when pushed to provide additional detail, they backed down. This worked out for me but didn't make the person making false claims happy. I didn't care, they were trying to build themselves up at my expense. Unfortunately, this particular company didn't have any concerns about people lying and acting this way—as you can imagine, I found a way out of that place.

The Judge—You Are Part of the Team, Just Not an Important Part—I once worked on a team where I knew I was contributing. I worked extra hours, did research on my own to understand the business and tried to soak in as much information as I could about what we did and how I could add value. Many people on the team acknowledged my dedication and even thanked me for it. There was a big meeting coming up and I was one of the contributors to an important presentation along with a handout that was going to be used as an informational marketing tool. One of the mid-level managers had the handout printed on fancy stock and there was a group of about 7-8 of us waiting to see it. This person passed them out to the group, then looked at me and literally said "no, you're not important enough," and snatched it back. Half of the team laughed; the other half didn't. I actually laughed and said OK, but it was very awkward and incredibly demoralizing. If there had been 20 people there and they said they only had 8 handouts, that would have been one thing (for the record, they had more) but to literally single me out as unimportant was just inappropriate. For context, it was early in my career, and I was the lowest titled person in the group. Later, after my boss had heard about this, they provided me a copy of the handout. I thanked them, but said it wasn't about having the handout, it was more about damaging my reputation in front of other people I needed to work with by being labeled unimportant. I never looked at the other manager the same again and although I'm a little embarrassed to admit it, their future requests usually ended up at the bottom of my to-do list. Don't be a judge; it's always OK to be nice to someone, regardless of title or status, and you don't want all your requests at the bottom of anyone's to-do list.

The Complicator—Some employees have figured out the secret to success is being the only one who understands how to do something and they purposefully keep things complicated so you can never replace them. This gives them comfort, but it also gives them some leverage. Make sure you always have someone who can step in and take over if needed—especially if it's a mission critical area or process. Having someone cross-trained to be able to step in is important and is the right thing to do for the company. I personally liked to have processes well documented "just in case"—the old "what happens if they get hit by a bus" scenario. Not everyone is going to want to do this (for obvious reasons) but it's important. It's also a great way to assure you have a well-defined process and people aren't just winging it. This documentation is also hard to argue with when someone wants special treatment or an exception. If you are the person who I described as holding on to information or making something complicated, I understand your motivation. As mentioned in another section of this book, this is not the recommended way to manage information and goes against most conventional thinking, but I've seen it work, and I get it.

The Drama Major—Drama is the worst. Everyone probably has some level of it and while most know how to keep it at arms-length, others breathe it in like oxygen. I'm going to keep this simple—you know that person who has an issue with everything or everyone and it's every day—they have a close relationship with misery, who we all know loves company. Do not align yourself with these people and definitely don't get pulled into their drama. It's going to be difficult if you are the type who empathizes and wants to help, but it is not going to benefit you; it's just going to wear you out and even worse may get you labeled with the drama tag, too. Give them guidance to leverage company or HR tools in place, and if these programs do not exist and you still want to help, you can suggest some independent external options. The most important thing is to make sure you don't make their problems your problems. I am not an unfeeling person, but the drama plague will infect you if you allow it.

The I Told You So—They are right; just ask them. They have an answer for everything and know better than everyone else how something should be done… sort of. Their hindsight is incredible, and they are not afraid to share it. When they see a difficult or complicated issue, they will boldly state that whatever it is will fail, and if it does, they proudly step forward and say, "I told you so." Their knowledge doesn't help solve problems, just highlights them and reminds everyone after the fact that they highlighted said problem. These people are terribly annoying. Once I have identified one of these people, I like to challenge them when they have a negative opinion about something; I specifically ask them what they think should be done. I commonly get the "not what they're doing" answer, which is an incredibly generic cop out. So, I push them to provide an actual suggestion. If they actually share one, I encourage them to take it to leadership. They never do and they usually stop telling me what they think after doing this—so, yay.

The Proclaimer—Provides direction with conviction only to change direction in a month or two. These people are incredibly reactive and latch onto the latest flavor of the month—often using catch phrases to try to sound knowledgeable but in reality, just end up sounding silly. I recall several proclaiming leaders who tried to "socialize" an idea throughout the company only to quickly backtrack. One example was the bold claim that the company would not save their way to profitability but instead would aggressively grow by expanding the customer base and selling additional products… After 6 months, the same leader told everyone to hold off on hiring any open positions and to cut their budgets to make sure the company could make their numbers. Proclaiming something, no matter how boldly, doesn't make it true or attainable. The changes desired in this example would require planning, investment, action, execution, and maybe even a cultural shift… not some empty proclamation. If nothing else has changed, other than a desire to be successful, it's unlikely you are going to be successful.

Can you imagine if this actually worked? I would be proclaiming things like tremendous success, a cure for cancer, winning the lottery, being taller, healthier, nicer, achieving world peace (not sure what it says about me that I put being taller ahead of world peace). There was another example when a company I was part of decided they wanted to have a moonshot-type goal. The company believed having such a goal would generate a broad-based employee rally behind it. The problem is, the culture of this company was not built to support such an endeavor. Instead of rallying everyone just rolled their eyes and waited for this latest fad to pass. It did. When leaders are championing ridiculous things that seem out of touch with reality, you may have little choice other than to agree with them, continue to do your job and pick up your check. If the culture is such that it embraces feedback, you may have more opportunity to share concerns but if it's a top down culture, you may want to think twice about being the messenger who potentially gets shot. Oh, and get used to corporate speak gibberish and non-sensical double talk – you are going to hear a lot of it.

The Complainer—No need to describe—we all know them. Don't be their fuel by agreeing with them. If you disagree, let them know you disagree—this may stop them from complaining to you in the future. If they don't stop, politely ask them to either be more positive or to not complain around you. Buy earplugs or headphones if you need to; you definitely don't want their negativity finding its way into your psyche. Here's something you could try: when I really want to tick off my wife, I'll wait until she's talking about something I have no interest in and tell her to wait a minute, then I'll put some earplugs in and tell her, OK, go ahead (I'm not as bad of a husband as that sounds like—she typically gives me a cross look or finds her way to my location and punches me… hard, which of course I deserve. The good news is if you are at work when you do this, they can't punch you). Even if you occasionally agree with what a complainer is saying, you don't want to be associated with them as you, too, may become known as a complainer. If you have a legitimate complaint about something, it will carry more weight if you pick your spots—if you complain about everything all the time you will eventually just be ignored. Oh, and don't actually do the earplug thing, even if you are at work, you will still likely get punched.

CHAPTER 17

There Is No Such Thing as a Lost Cause...or Is There?

I F YOU ARE A DECENT HUMAN BEING, BY DEFAULT YOU MAY naturally want to help people, but sometimes you simply can't... don't allow a lost cause to consume all of your time. For every one time someone was able to turn their situation around, there are at least another ten times when they couldn't. There can be a lot of reasons someone isn't performing well—it can be home or other personal challenges, substance issues, skill set deficiencies, personality clashes, low motivation...the list is long.

My personal belief is that you should try to help, even if the odds are against you, but realize you can only do so much. I watched a manager try to coach and help an individual, who just wasn't good at their job, improve their skills. The person was good at the job before it grew into something more, but after it evolved and required greater understanding of more sophisticated tools, they really struggled. The manager was patient, provided training, and even sat with them to do 1 on 1 work sessions to try to help them. This manager was determined to make this person good at their job! The problem was, they simply weren't going to be good at it. When the role was more support in nature, they were capable, but when it became 50% technical, they were out of their element. No amount of time was going to change their internal wiring. They were smart but this just wasn't their cup of tea (would be like me trying to do an Engineering job, it's just not going to happen). Both the manager and employee should have understood the eventual outcome and worked to find a more appropriate role for the person but instead they spent months trying to force a square peg into a round hole. The employee needed support from everyone on the team, including the manager, and was a real drag on productivity. Eventually, frustration by others created animosity and team morale degraded. The employee was eventually let go after a long and tedious effort to try to reshape them into something they weren't. I'm not sure how everyone except the manager was able to see there was no hope, but the significant amount of time and energy spent to try to get this person qualified for their job was overkill when it was clearly a hopeless cause. Some of this will come with experience but knowing when to pull the plug can save you and the company a lot of frustration and wasted time. Trying to help is OK, but understand you are not obligated to try forever. The individual also needs to take accountability—in this example, they should have seen the writing on the wall and been looking for a different role that was better aligned with their capabilities.

There was another situation where an employee left one department to join another. The hiring manager knew there were some skill related shortcomings but convinced themselves that the person would "learn" the position once onboard. Within 2 days, the employee knew…

1 They were never going to be able to do the job, and

2 Having other people help them all the time was going to create friction.

3 The employee and manager worked together and with HR's help, found a new role that better fit their skills. All of this could have been avoided if either hiring manager or employee had done a better job understanding the role up front; but I think it was a little bit of the employee trying to get out of their current situation and the manager desperately needing a "warm body." Bonus lesson: take time and hire the right person, which may not necessarily be the first person.

Trust, But Verify.... I had a manager who could have avoided hiring a lost cause but didn't. Here's what happened: an area under my umbrella of responsibility needed to backfill an open position, so we posted for the role internally and received a few interested candidates. I suggested the manager with the open position call the current manager of the top candidate we were considering, and to also check with HR to see if they could read over their performance reviews. The candidate's current manager was contacted and provided a glowing review and even asked what type of work the person would be doing. They said it would be a great fit and would be a big win for our team. Well, the manager on my team didn't read the performance reviews and if they had done a little additional due diligence, they would have discovered that the person was known by everyone on the current team to be difficult to work with, created headwind for others and generated unnecessary drama.

A couple of things to take away from this: first, be thorough when bringing someone on to your team. If they are an internal candidate, there may actually be insight you can gain through informal channels. Taking on someone else's problems is a nightmare—the previous manager never should have dumped their problems on someone else. Perhaps there was a challenge trying to manage them out or they didn't want to deal with it and they figured it was easier to just pass the buck. Here's the deal—take responsibility and handle your own difficult issues. It's a coward's move to ship your problems off to someone else. If you provide full information to another manager first, and they still want the person, then that's on them; but dumping your problems will only breed a distrust for you and it could damage your reputation. I never trusted the manager who provided the glowing review again and even maintained a personal bias against them for being less than honest.

CHAPTER 18

I'm Going to Let This Call Go to Voicemail...

THE TITLE OF THIS SECTION IS EXACTLY WHAT I USED TO SAY when a specific person would call. Difficult people can drain you, but you're going to have to learn how to deal with them because there simply is no shortage of them and it would be ridiculous to think that you will never cross paths with one. There was one individual who had a reputation of regularly asking for the ridiculous and impossible. Every solution, no matter how good, needed to be improved and they thought their opinions represented the opinions of everyone else. It was funny; when they called, you would hear the phones in other offices ring, then stop... another one would ring, then another... until it eventually found its way to me. I don't know if I should be flattered that the call eventually came my way or insulted that they tried so many others first... regardless, I would always take their call, even though I knew they were going to be a real handful. I viewed it as a challenge and would tell myself "if I can resolve this, I can handle anything." Eventually the ringing in other offices stopped and they would just start with me (knowing I would pick up the phone). I found a way to build a relationship with this person, helped them understand a perspective different from theirs and eventually gained their trust, respect and support. I was also the savior of every other person who didn't want to take their call. I remember being at a large conference-type meeting and an executive came up to me and said something to the effect of "… not sure what you're doing, but so and so thinks you are wonderful, which is high praise."

I don't like dealing with difficult people any more than the next person, but you can't be afraid. There is always going to be someone difficult to deal with and the more experience you have dealing with them, the better you will be able to handle those situations at work and in your home life. Keep in mind, although they don't know it, these people are difficult all of the time. It's how they are wired, so they are good at it— you need to get good at dealing with them or you will be at a disadvantage every time you come across one. Don't fear talking to anyone, you will likely grow from the experience.

CHAPTER 19

Stuff for Leaders to Consider....

LEADING IS NOT A DEMOCRATIC ACTIVITY; YOU CAN ASK FOR AND receive input without having to act on it. It seems like new leaders in particular feel compelled to solicit input from their team. They also may feel like they have to implement the team's suggestions. Remember, other people's perspective is not the same as yours. Those who do not have to make an actual decision will always have suggestions, as those suggestions are immune from failure and any repercussions. If you are the one who has to make or present a decision and are going to have to live with the outcome, you get to determine what that final decision is. It's definitely OK to get input, and that input will let the team know you value their opinions, and it may even be helpful, but you need to filter the parts that are relevant. Ultimately, you are going to be responsible for the decisions you make. Having other points of view or perspectives is fine, but they should be used to inform, not specifically act upon.

...Can We Just Skip This Part

People should be provided opportunity to grow, develop, shine and be recognized for their work. I think it's appropriate for them to want greater exposure and to have access to other leaders in the company but they (or you) should not try to do this without working in conjunction with their manager.

Here's one approach to how to handle this: I had a couple of my really good bosses who conducted regular skip level development meetings with staff reporting to their direct reports… in other words, my boss would meet regularly in a 1:1 session with my direct reports. This provides broader exposure and a potential development path for people who wanted it and helped the team feel like they were being heard by management. As a manager, I liked having my staff get this opportunity. It kept me involved in their development and at times they would even want to meet with me first to create a plan of how to best utilize their time with the big boss. For those who felt like they needed to show how smart they were, it gave them a forum without having to "go around" me, and in some cases validated, for my boss, the challenges I had with certain employees. A good boss will help reinforce behavioral expectations, and this is a great approach to help with that. It also allowed the big boss to better understand what individuals on the team did. In short order, I learned to have zero concern when my boss would go directly to someone on the team instead of through me for something—they knew the team and I welcomed the engagement. If you are looking for a way to get broader exposure, you may want to introduce this concept to your boss. Be sure to lay out the benefits… a good boss should not have any issues with wanting to do this.

Conversely, there may be times when a boss doesn't want to develop people on their team or provide access for their employees—maybe because they are too focused on themselves, are so busy it's not on their mind, they are afraid if they develop you they may lose you, or if they develop you, you may be better positioned to take their job. If this is your situation, you may want to see if there are other paths for you. One option is to work "around" your boss on your own, but that may earn you a reputation (and not the good kind). You definitely don't want to be known as the person who goes around their boss—if you get that moniker, no one will want you. In a perfect world you should be able to reach out to anyone, but the world we live in is far from perfect. One approach may be to volunteer for initiatives or projects that are championed by leaders in the company—they may be for things like community outreach or other company supported programs or charitable work. This is a great way to meet new people, give back to the community and still show off your skills. Don't underestimate the value of this kind of engagement.

Here's How I Know If Someone Is a Good Leader: the people they manage are fiercely loyal, would leave a higher paying job to work for them, and an implicit level of trust exists. People working for good leaders also tend to do the best work they've ever done and do more than they thought they could do. They go the extra mile when needed and it is not uncommon for them to also model the leader's behavior and eventually become a good leader in their own right. The leader thinks of the people first, then the team, then of course the company. They understand without the people the company has no soul. I once asked a team member why they made the decision they made and their answer was "I thought about what your decision would be and did that." A kind and humbling comment to receive. I'm not suggesting I was always a good leader, but I had my moments. The idea is to stitch as many of those moments together as you can, and before you know it, you are leading instead of just managing. Have some patience, if you are like me you may need to evolve into a leader over time. It also helps if you have managers that provide opportunities to learn and improve. If you make a mistake along the way, learn from it and don't make it again.

If You Are an Individual Contributor.... Contribute—don't be afraid to share your thoughts and opinions, especially when asked. Working with a given situation or with data, information, tools, or other people and teams provides you with a valuable perspective that your manager may not have. Having an opinion based on that perspective can be helpful to your manager. Keep in mind, your perspective may be helpful but is only your perspective, so don't take it too personally if your ideas aren't always used. Remember, a manager needs to hear all sides of a situation, then determine the best course of action based on what may be additional information you aren't privy to. Even if your suggestions are not followed, keep making them, as it shows you are engaged, thinking about how to improve things and exhibits a willingness to contribute. If all your suggestions are always used—that's great—but it also may indicate that you have a better grasp on the business than your boss. This can definitely happen, and it probably means you are ready for the next step in your career.

Providing input does come with potential risk. If a manager takes your input and makes a decision based on it, and that decision turns out to be a bad one, a poor manager may come back and shoot the messenger…i.e., you (not literally shoot you, but blame you since it was your idea. If you are concerned that your manager may actually shoot you, it's time to find a new job!) They could also lose confidence or trust in you. This is on them, not you. They need to know how to take disparate information and distill it for decision making. If you are continually being punished as the messenger, you probably have a bad manager and you may want to be more careful in how you provide input. For example, you may want to literally say something like "with the limited information I have available to me, and from my perspective, it looks like XYZ, but will defer to you to determine how to best interpret that." This may seem a little cowardly, and I'm not suggesting to always do this, but if your manager has a history of assigning blame, you may want to find ways to protect yourself. Conversely, if you consistently provide input, information and feedback that garners praise for your manger, but that praise never trickles down to you, and you are not reaping any benefit (promotion, raise, more responsibility, etc.), you should consider asking for the recognition you earned. A selfish manager may be reluctant, but you should still ask. It's ok to be a team player, but if you are contributing to team or company success, you should get credit.

CHAPTER 20

Yes, There Are Bad Leaders

This is a story about an experience with one:

I HAD TO PUT TOGETHER A PROGRAM FOR A BIG MEETING, AND BY program, I mean the piece of paper folded in half that has the times of each event listed, along with the names of the people leading those events. I had listed individual names and one of the leaders presenting had one of those names that could be listed either formally or informally, with a couple of different ways to spell it. I looked the person up in the company directory to make sure I had it listed correctly (which I later found out was not listed correctly in the directory) and in addition, asked their administrative assistant to review and confirm the name was correct. In hindsight, I discovered the assistant didn't really look very closely and just said it was OK. So, the design was sent to the marketing people and they put together the document.

I arrived at the event several hours early to help set up the room and lay the programs out on the table and lucky me, I bumped into this leader. They asked to see the program, so I showed it to them. They told me their name was spelled incorrectly. I was beside myself and said something to the effect of "oh no, I'm sorry that happened, what part of it is incorrect?" While tossing the program, they said to me, you figure it out... and added, get it fixed. I only had a couple of hours to get everything reprinted and we were already off site at the meeting loca-tion (same town, but off site at a hotel). After being given the directive to correct the error, but still not knowing what the error was, I decided to give my boss a heads-up and asked if they could identify the issue. They decided to help me and asked this particular person what the error was, but the person decided they didn't want to tell my boss what was wrong either (a real team player). I called the admin and discovered the person in question didn't like the spelling we used, even though that was the way it was in the directory. They suggested I use their formal name instead. I gave my boss another heads up, got the OK and went with the formal name. I had to call the marketing people to clear the decks so another version of the program could be expeditiously reprinted, then I had to quickly go back to the corporate office, pick up the changes and bring them to the hotel where the meeting was being held. I pulled it off! That "leader" saw me and asked if I figured out the error. Trying to diffuse a tense situation, I jokingly said I realized I hadn't hyphenated their name (and was going to say just kidding and explain what I had changed) but before I could say anything, they grabbed at one of the programs I was holding and looked at the now corrected name. They then gave me a death stare and slowly raised their hand while flipping me off. Later in the evening, part of their presentation was about teamwork and helping each other succeed... so incredibly hypocritical.

I wish the name had been correct, and I was sorry the mistake hap-pened and was willing to fix it, but the way they handled the entire situ-ation was less than professional, especially by someone who is supposed to be modeling leadership behavior. I always maintained positive rela-tionships with the people who reported to this person, so there should not have been any reason to treat me poorly other than the fact that they could, so they did. I may have just been a pawn in a larger battle, as this person didn't like one of the leaders in the area I worked, so whatever they could do to undermine that area was fair game. What's funny is this wasn't even my job; I was just helping out in a short-handed situation. Someone who feels like they can bully other people tells me all I need to know about them. If you are being bullied by someone who is sup-posed to be a leader, find ways to avoid working with that person; they are consumers of energy and sanity and whatever you do will never be good enough for them. You have more control than you think in how you allow other people to engage with you.

That Was Fun, Let's Do Another One... I worked a few jobs where a company loved an outside consultant so much, they would hire them after an engagement ended. Some consultants transition well, but some don't. Identifying issues and making boiler plate suggestions for change is not the same as implementing, managing, operationalizing and living with those changes. In one of the examples where the person was not successful transitioning, they continued to be in consultant mode instead of business owner mode. They also brought some of their own people in from outside, which may work, and even help breathe fresh perspectives into a culture, but unfortunately it can also poison one. In the example I'm describing, it was poison. The people brought in were previously lower level staff employees who were elevated above their capabilities and acted as extensions of the leader (some staff actually referred to them as spies... that is never a good thing). I didn't think they were spies, but I did worry about the now idiot deprived villages they came from.

The internal staff person who probably should have received the leadership role was seen as a threat and did not play along with the new leader's shenanigans, so they were seen as a problem. The issue here is this: the person who should have received the role was the one who re-ally knew what was going on, how to navigate the organization, had es-tablished positive relationships and had a good reputation. Now, they were treated like the enemy. They worked hard to help build an area that was handed over to someone else who had no clue. By the way, the exec-utive who hired the external leader was soon after let go for... let's just say, "bad things." I viewed the new leader as narcissistic and they used their position to intimidate and bully people. Everyone knew this, yet it was allowed. I've seen this at more than one company and sadly many times (i.e., a new leader is given some latitude to try to do things their way, regardless if it's contrary to corporate culture or so-called values). Even when loyal company first employees raised issues, their concerns were dismissed or put on the back burner. This was one of those times I knew I could wait out a bad situation—this was a classic scorpion and frog story; I knew this person's nature was to sting. They were abrasive, rude and even demeaning to people. They were also insanely bold in not caring who saw their behavior. They were smart enough to behave a little better in front of senior leadership, but as with all narcissistic egomaniacs (and I'm being kind in my description) they eventually imploded. They were gone, and the flying monkeys they brought with them soon followed. The role was given to the person who originally should have been promoted, and they reestablished balance to the department. Such an unnecessary mess.

I recall another executive who was let go, and the day (night) prior to leaving, they went out and had a big night on the town with their team and expensed the whole thing. I was actually there but didn't partake in any of the extravagancies like shots of very old and very expensive liquor or imported cigars. I ate a basic meal, not the steak and lobster others had, and did my best to stay above the fray. Some of the participants were reprimanded, while others were not—this kind of inconsistency wreaks havoc with trust. Remember, do as I say, not as I do.

And One More… I had someone basically pick a verbal fight with me in a large meeting. They were several levels above me and were recommending a terrible idea (which I later assume was on purpose). I made my case in a polite way and suggested we table the decision until we could all get on the same page. I actually had people who reported to this turd… I mean, individual, come up to me after the meeting to apologize for this person's behavior. I told them it wasn't their responsibility to do that but I appreciated their willingness to reach out to me.

As it turns out, and with the luxury of hindsight, I discovered this person had another opportunity outside the company and the word was if they got fired they would be eligible for a separation package. The meeting was related to an expensive and visible project, so it made sense to target this type of setting. Well, I shouldn't have felt so special; over the next two weeks this person "picked fights" with several other people related to high profile projects and was successful in getting fired... I mean, "decided to pursue other opportunities." When something seems outrageous or out of left field, there may be ulterior motives. If someone is pushing your buttons to try to get a reaction, don't give them the satisfaction. Unless you work in a life or death profession that requires immediate action, don't overreact to something that catches you off guard—take a deep breath and stay calm until you can step away and rationally evaluate the situation with emotion removed.

A quick editorial comment — 90% of my career was filled with positive experiences, I'm sharing the ones that you may not see coming or be prepared for... but can still happen.

CHAPTER 21

Silly Things

COMPANIES ARE COMPRISED OF PEOPLE, AND PEOPLE CAN overthink things, which means companies can overthink things.

They may take what you perceive to be odd actions. These actions are taken because they want to look like they have their act together for their customers, investors, employees… or it may be to position themselves from a legal standpoint—who knows. Whatever the reason, companies will sometimes do what I consider silly things. For example, I have always found it humorous when a company releases a statement (internal or external) about people who leave "to pursue other opportunities." Like no one knows what that means… and by the way, everyone talks, so there really are no secrets.

I've also attended more than one "retirement" party for people only to see them start a job at a different company the following week. Maybe there was a financial incentive for them to call it "retirement" not sure— but how absurd. I had one boss leave a company and prior to their departure, they went on a road show for all their teams to say goodbye (why this was allowed is a mystery to me). They forgot my team in the roadshow, which they realized a few hours into their last day. They felt compelled to hastily throw together one final meeting to leave us with some inspirational words of wisdom. Every person in the room knew they were invited as an afterthought; I mean, come on—they literally forgot about us! After some grandstanding met with lots of eye rolls, the meeting ended and the person left, never to be thought of again. The main point here is to understand there will be times you just have to roll with things that seem ridiculous. Even high-titled people are human and can over-react or overthink things when stressed. Regardless of what level or title someone has achieved, when faced with a new and challenging situation, they may not know how to handle it. Sometimes, human nature takes over as common sense disappears. My suggestion to you is this: when things seem their craziest, take a deep breath and rely on common sense.

CHAPTER 22

When You Work In A "Do As I Say, Not As I Do" Culture

I F THIS IS YOUR SITUATION, YOU WILL NEED TO EITHER ADJUST and be ok with it or look for a way out.

Many companies have boxes they need to check to show their progressive stance on values, diversity & inclusion, community involvement, work-life balance, whatever the current hot topic is. Sometimes corporate values are only meant for employees, not management... well, maybe some management, but not all management. Actually, some staff are immune, too—it really depends on who you are, who you know, and how "valuable" you are deemed to be.

When I Said We, I Meant You...

At multiple companies, I implemented tools and solutions for various teams to use. In one of these companies, the tool(s) were endorsed by leadership and rank & file employees were directed to use them. They were told that the investment in these platforms was substantial & important and the company had fully embraced the tools along with the new philosophy and processes they helped to support. It was even further iterated that everyone, including leadership, would use the new tools, and there would be no exceptions. Can you guess where this is going? To start, leaders didn't show up to training, so right away staff felt like the utilization of the new tools was optional. In some cases, we had to schedule additional training just for individual leaders—not enough time to actually train them, just enough for them to say they went through training. A quick check of the login history showed that leadership almost never used the tools. Some of the solutions I am talking about (I believe) would have been adopted much quicker if leaders practiced a little more what they preached. They didn't need to become power users; just a casual user that occasionally utilized the tools. If their staff saw this, it would have sent a clear message that the tools were important. Don't tell everyone about a new solution (and how important it is) if you don't plan on actually using it yourself.

Unfortunately, if you are responsible for implementing something new that requires adoption, you may have a difficult time getting buy in. If everyone is clamoring for it, you may have an easier path, but do everything you can to get leaders to actually lead on these types of initiatives. When the top is bought in it makes trickle down adoption much easier.

Know the Culture… If you know documented cultural and/or value statements are just words or false programs & initiatives and not the actual culture, you will be OK. If you swallowed the culture story hook, line & sinker and believe it's real, then discover it isn't, you are going to feel foolish, deceived and disappointed.

You also need to be aware that all the documented cultural and value statements can, and will, be used to judge you when beneficial to the company. For example, if they want or need to justify why you didn't get a promotion or raise, or justification for why you were reorganized out of a job—they can create pretty much whatever narrative they want, whenever they want, and may use these "values" in order to do so. There are countless examples of companies paying extravagant consulting fees to put together a set of values or competencies, or whatever the latest buzz phrase is, to look good to regulators or the public—but that doesn't mean that's how they really act or conduct business.

There are some companies that truly live the values they publish, but I'm not sure that's the norm. My position has always been to just be honest about who you are. I've worked at places that acted the polar op-posite of what they said they were on paper. This can become problem-atic when the "rules" are loosely followed and broadly interpreted based on who you are. I wish companies would just write the value set to re-flect who they truly are; then no one would be disappointed. Remember, simply saying something is true doesn't make it true… actions really are the best measure.

Some companies really do live the culture and values they publish, but whether a company lives them or not, you should still do your part to adhere to them; they are probably worthy values, and you don't want to give a company any reason to eliminate your job.

CHAPTER 23

A Compass Can Be Helpful

I LEARNED MUCH TOO LATE IN MY CAREER HOW IMPORTANT IT IS TO have an advocate to help you grow through advice, introductions, championing, mentoring and general guidance. I had some good managers who weren't mentors or advocates. I learned from them, but not because they specifically taught me something, rather I had to watch them and pick things up as I went along. It's kind of like trying to learn how to use a software package by reading about it vs. having someone sit down and show you, allowing you to ask questions and get real time feedback. Some people may be great at learning by just reading or passively watching, but like many people, I am more of a hands-on type of person and find it helpful to receive real time feedback as well as understand the thought process related to decision making.

For some time, I wouldn't know how my work was being used at the next level; it was just assigned and produced. Asking questions would help a little, but more often than not I would simply be given some generic business speak that made no sense. I understood that some of this would come with experience and I didn't expect to learn everything in a couple of weeks; however, the learning curve could have been accelerated exponentially if there was someone that could have helped guide me along the way. I take responsibility for this, as I didn't specifically search out an advocate or mentor, I was waiting for it to organically happen. I did have a few opportunities that I should have pursued, but didn't pro-actively take advantage of them — shame on me.

Definitely try to establish a relationship with a mentor and/or ad-vocate. They may happen upon you, but more likely you will need to seek them out. Not all mentor relationships will work out, but if you don't try you won't know. When you do establish a mentor / mentee re-lationship, please don't make it all about you. I've seen examples where a mentee would target someone they believed could get them promoted and basically spent all their time explaining why they were so deserv-ing of a promotion. This can be pretty transparent, and needless to say, those types of relationships usually don't work out. If you want to learn, a good leader will usually be willing to teach. If you just want to ingrati-ate yourself with someone, they will likely see through it and instead of having an advocate you may end up with a detractor. For those of you who are leaders, take the time to invest in someone else—this could be the most rewarding work you do. I can guarantee you won't remember the weekly TPS reports, but a good mentor/mentee relationship can stay with you forever.

…And Don't Miss a Chance to Leverage Opportunity

At one job, I was selected for a development program that identified fu-ture leaders of the company. I attended a weeklong off-site session, where I was well received and could have, and should have, leveraged that ex-perience and those relationships into something more than I did. At the end of the program, the participants were asked to present findings of a team project we were assigned. I was selected to be one of the pre-senters, and I did pretty well. I was comfortable with the material and knew what I was talking about, so I was comfortable presenting. I can't stress how important this is—if you know your topic, you will come across as relaxed and credible. Anyway, here was another "miss." I could have leveraged this new network and the now-known skill of "present-ing" into something more, but I didn't. To give myself a little credit, I was always a pretty good presenter, but the introverted part of me just doesn't love doing it. Instead, I have always been happy contributing behind the scenes and didn't feel I needed the spotlight. The problem with this thinking is that it's the spotlight that allows you to be seen. So, life lesson learned—if you have a network you can tap into or a skill that differentiates you, use it.

CHAPTER 24

Surround Yourself With Quality People

THIS IS TRUE FOR YOUR WORK AND PERSONAL LIFE. YOU MAY HAVE heard the term misery loves company... it can be true, but the other saying that can also be true is success breeds success. In the former, if all you have around you is failure and despair, there's a pretty good chance you are going to find yourself failing and desperate. Not always the case, but when there is no one to lift you up, and you are only exposed to the negative side of life, it makes everything more difficult. If, on the other hand, there is nothing but success around you, success will seem normal and expected. You will see how successful people handle themselves and will probably learn from them. Those who started out surrounded by misery can absolutely break free of that life and compete with those blessed with successful surroundings, but it's a lot easier when you're not already overwhelmed by negativity.

I was raised in a small town outside of Pittsburgh where a lot of families were blue-collar and for a good stretch of my youth, out of work. My perspective was pretty narrow and my goal was to get out of high school and get a job. Not a good job, or a job with a chance for advancement, or doing something that inspired me —just a job. I watched my family struggle to make mortgage payments, car payments, you-name-it payments. I knew how to float a check before I had a checking account and looked up to role models that, by any measure, were no such thing.

Jumping from one job to another was normal, and I always expected to be an employee in some labor-intensive role. College was never a consideration and owning a home was unlikely. A few things happened that changed this path for me:

1   I had some really awful jobs that made me rethink the idea that any job was a good job—I believed there had to be something more.

2   I was hanging around some low-quality people who I knew were low quality. I was pretty sure life could be better.

3   I met some successful people and discovered that although they may have been more successful than me, they were no smarter… so I figured that maybe I could be successful, too.

4   I had someone I respected tell me I was smart enough to do more than I was doing, and that an education would open doors for me.

In other sections in this book I talk about number 1 from above, no need to rehash here.

In the second example, it was a misery-loves-company situation. I think there are times people want to feel like they are not alone, so finding others who are struggling makes them feel "normal." Don't fall into this trap. Find positive people; remove drama from your life and work to find places and people who build you up. Life isn't always going to be puppy dogs and rainbows, but it's easier to deal with the occasional crap sandwiches life is going to hand you when everything else around you isn't also crap.

For the third example, I had a few happenstance opportunities to meet some successful people and discovered the only thing they had going for them that I didn't was opportunity, and most of them had a college education (which helped create opportunity). By the way, I still think college is important, but not sure it is the only type of "education" that can launch a career in today's world. I know some technical/IT types who have no college education but who I would certainly describe as educated and often the smartest person in the room... even a room with ivy league graduates. The college vs. skills debate is interesting, and I can argue either side of the coin. Skills seem to be almost as important now as a college degree, although I could make the case that many of those skills can and will be obtained in college.

Having someone who you respect in your corner is pretty important and can change your course. Hearing supportive words is always nice but hearing them from someone who's opinion matters to you can be meaningful, impactful and may inspire you to do more than you thought you could. You never know who may look up to you, so don't be afraid to share positive feedback when the opportunity presents itself. When someone realizes they have access to the same tools to achieve success as everyone else, it can be life altering.

Here's a quick story about some quality people I've worked with. I was a manager of a team that was filled with highly skilled, highly motivated people who needed little guidance. I was an experienced manager, so there were no feelings of insecurity by having super capable and smart people to manage; rather, it made life so much easier. The team was comprised of both internal staff as well as consultants and contractors, and the only real challenge was keeping other people from consuming their time... and me staying out of their way after providing direction. I would receive updates, ask for potential issues, backup plans, resource constraints... all of which were already considered and planned for. One time, before a big project was about to launch, and after it was confirmed that everyone had everything covered, I simply said—"OK, don't screw up." I'm not sure why I said it, but what I meant was everyone there was very good at their jobs and if everyone did what they were supposed to do we were going to be successful... and we were. It sort of became a thing, and right before each project, no one would leave the planning meeting until I said it. It was our version of "break a leg."

Here's a fact—smart people make life more interesting; I learned something from people on this team every day. I remember telling them that they should really embrace and enjoy this window in time we were all experiencing; having such a capable and collaborative team delivering high quality work with a level of mutual respect is a rare thing. Sadly, the team was eventually folded into another department within the company during a restructuring... there are kingdoms to be built, power struggles to be won, egos to stroke and titles to justify. It's OK to have capable people who don't need your help every 10 minutes. If you have this scenario, embrace it and be thankful; it really is an extraordinary and amazing thing. By the way, even though I no longer work with these people, I keep in touch with many of them. They proactively reach out to me, and I proactively reach out to them. We all cheer for each other and are excited when we get to connect in person. People who want to see you succeed are people you want in your life.

As Long as We're Talking About People... I know it's hard to believe, but not all people are of high quality and this is why you should always consider the source. It never hurts to listen, but listening doesn't always mean you have to act. You may want to first determine if what X person tells you is consistently good advice or not. If it is, you may want to consider listening to their suggestions, if not... well, don't. I always use my internal voice and tell myself "consider the source." For example, if the source is reliable and has a consistent track record of being helpful, kind and fair and that person gives you less than terrific feedback about something, you may want to take a look inward because they are probably just being honest and trying to help you. If the source is always complaining, never takes accountability and has a reputation for being difficult, selfish, mean or any other negative attributes, you are probably OK to dismiss them. I've taken to heart too many things from sources I didn't respect and shouldn't have listened to. Don't let this happen to you. If I practice a speech and my wife tells me it's not very good, I listen... because she's smart, but I also know she has my best interest in mind—she doesn't want me to look bad. She's a good source to listen to. The lesson here is: if my wife gives you feedback, take it... oh, and consider the source.

CHAPTER 25

Get Engaged

NOT ENGAGED LIKE GETTING MARRIED, ALTHOUGH THAT'S FINE, too—but engaged with people, activities, something. A book club, a sport, a hobby—it doesn't matter, but keep your mind and body active. Idle hands make no cookies... OK, that's not a real saying, and I don't even know what it means, but my point is it's easy to fall into the trap of: go to work, come home, eat dinner, entertain yourself with a show or social media, go to bed.... or even worse, come home, work some more, go to bed.

And don't just consume; find a way to contribute. It may be hard at first, especially if you are not naturally comfortable engaging with others. But with today's technology you can do things online and across the planet without ever having to see anyone in person. Play chess with an opponent in another country or join an online forum discussing ways to help local shelters improve conditions for animals in their care. Whatever it is that you are passionate about and enjoy, take (and make) time to enjoy it.

In twenty years, you are not going to remember skipping an episode of some reality show or who "liked" what on social media (you won't even remember it next week). Connecting with other humans is important. Doing actual things is important. Getting out into nature is important. Make time to do these things, either alone, or with family and friends—but do something. I personally believe connecting with animals is important too—if you have the time and money needed to properly care for an animal, I'm sure there is a shelter near you that would be happy to introduce you to some of their guests. If you decide to adopt a pet, remember puppies and kittens are great, but older pets need homes, too.

CHAPTER 26

Stuck a Feather in My Hat and Called It... Success

WHEN SOMETHING GOOD HAPPENS ON YOUR TEAM LIKE A BIG project gets completed or you finished a really hard assignment, congratulate yourself and/or the team. I know; it's your job and you get paid to do it, but some work requires extra effort or takes especially long to complete, so it's nice to mark the occasion. I don't think you need to celebrate the fact that you successfully logged onto the network in the morning—make sure it's something worth recognition—but don't just let it pass. Also, do it relatively close to the time it happens; you don't want to celebrate something from six months ago—a lot can happen in-between that time.

The celebration doesn't have to be expensive or fancy, just an opportunity to show appreciation for each other and recognize an accomplishment or a job well done. Definitely don't force it; no one likes to be told to have fun (that brings back some old memories of childhood). It can be as simple as cupcakes for the team during an afternoon break or getting a conference room and having a brown bag lunch and go-around acknowledging what everyone contributed. By the way, it's OK to invite members of an extended team, as well—that's a great way to build camaraderie.

One time I had a person on my team who shared that in their culture they were given a feather for their hat to recognize an accomplishment. So, after one of our big projects I brought in a hat with a feather to place on the table next to a celebratory cake. To my surprise, people started to spontaneously wear the hat, and we all took pictures wearing it (the next time, I just bought everyone their own hat because you never really know individual hygiene practices… but I digress). After that, it became a regular thing to share feathers for successful projects. This speaks to the culture of appreciating each other as people and for the effort everyone contributes. It sure makes for a more pleasant workplace when people enjoy what they do and even better if they enjoy who they do it with. Some companies have specific recognition programs, which are nice, but they may have some hurdles to clear in order to "award" the actual recognition. It may also limit who or how many can be recognized. I definitely think using established programs is helpful, but also believe there is something to doing your own thing once in a while. Do be careful not to turn it into a secondary company program, as this may be frowned upon. Use your best judgment, but if you aren't using company funds for any of it, I'm guessing you'll be OK.

A Different Kind of Celebration

As long as we are on the topic of celebrating, I should mention that it's also OK to celebrate and congratulate individuals on achievements—they can be work-related or even personal achievements. When you get promoted, you are happy, and you want others to be happy for you. If you are never happy for anyone else, there's a pretty good chance they are never going to be happy for you, either. We've all seen undeserving people get promoted, but there are also times when very deserving people get promoted. It's possible multiple people are deserving, but only one can get the job. Being disappointed that you didn't get a job and being happy for someone else that did aren't mutually exclusive things. If you are upset about a promotion, it's not going to benefit anyone by saying something bad behind their back. In these cases, use the "if you don't have anything nice to say, don't say any-thing" approach. Being negative or upset will likely just make you look petty and childish. You need to congratulate others when they achieve success—period. This will also be necessary if you have any interest in having others congratulate you on your accomplishments.

CHAPTER 27

Out of My Way, Old-Timer—I Have Some Fresh Ideas

I F YOU ARE THE YOUNG UPSTART WHO HAS SOME GREAT IDEAS AND you just need the old-timers who have been at the company forever to get out of your way, cool your jets a little. Markets can, and do, change and sometimes new innovation can be introduced to enhance and improve an offering, but what you think is a fresh perspective may just be another attempt of the same old thing. A former colleague and I laugh about how often old initiatives are dusted off and retried, often without any clue that it had been tried before. If you are trying something that you believe is new, don't dismiss feedback from others that may have tried "it" before. There is no shame in learning from the past. For the record, having tried before doesn't mean it shouldn't be tried again—it could be the market wasn't ready, the execution was poor, it didn't have strategic support, it competed with other initiatives that overshadowed it, regulatory challenges existed that are no longer in place, the list goes on. Try to understand why it wasn't successful the first (or second) time around—it may help you achieve success this time around. In addition, don't just assume it failed because you weren't part of the team. As smart as you are, you're probably not that much smarter than everyone else, so keep your hat size in check.

If you are the "old-timer", don't rain on their parade. Fresh perspective, excitement and enthusiasm are not bad things. Do your best to be supportive and provide insight as to what was done in the past and the challenges associated with it. It is possible that the timing is now better, the technology to support the initiative has evolved, or perhaps the stars have just finally aligned for success. If it seemed like a good idea before, and still does, maybe it is. If you know something is going to fail because it failed three previous times, and nothing has changed, you should probably say something, but if the dynamics of the market or product have changed and it looks like it could be successful, it may be worthy of support and another attempt.

Deep down you may be secretly wishing for failure again just to validate that it wasn't your fault the first time around (hopefully you are not really wishing this) but you really should try to help—your history with an endeavor like this may be the difference between failure and success.

CHAPTER 28

A Barrel Full of Monkeys...

WORKED AT A COUPLE OF COMPANIES WHERE THE AREAS I WORKED in were in super-growth mode. Even better, every project we undertook was successful; wow, were we smart! A little hindsight has helped me understand that although the work we were doing was good, and everyone on the team was smart and capable, we were also lucky to be in the right place at the right time. The reality is anyone with some smarts and a willingness to work hard would have also been successful. I now joke that a monkey could have thrown a dart at ideas and whichever one it hit would have worked. Looking back, I really should have better leveraged the good will that came with being part of a super successful team. Participating in that hyper growth environment exposed me to new experiences faster than some of my contemporaries. That accelerated learning curve is something I should have packaged and taken on to greener pastures. I did continue to slowly grow and advance in my career, but should have seen this as an opportunity to embrace something new while "in demand". There are no guarantees, but given my knowledge, work ethic and drive, I believe moving on to something new could have accelerated my professional growth. I could have gone and thrown darts... I mean, implemented other great ideas somewhere else – this is a missed opportunity that could have helped establish an even better reputation and made me more marketable.

I've also seen the opposite happen: everything a person touches fails, but they keep getting new opportunities, and maybe even promoted. How does this happen? On one hand, it may not be their fault. Some areas are just not going to succeed regardless of who's in charge. At some point, even the smartest person in the world wasn't going to save Blockbuster video after the market changed (younger readers, you may need to look this up). It could also be that a company wants their best person trying "new" things—this person may be smart, has done something similar before and is comfortable working with the unknown. One could argue that an area may have failed, but with anyone else running it, it could have been X times worse. This person's job may be to try new things, and even fail, but to understand and be comfortable with "failing quickly" and knowing when to cut the cord. There are many legitimate reasons this situation may exist. On the other hand, they may just have connections with people who continue to provide them opportunity because they, their kids, or their spouses are friends. It doesn't really matter. What does matter is that they are in a leadership role in this area of the company and you may need to work with them.

Working in one of these speculative or startup areas can be very rewarding, especially if you are able to "hit" on a successful endeavor. Being part of something new can be incredibly exciting as well as provide opportunity to grow professionally as the area grows, or maybe even explodes - this may be your ticket to fast professional development and advancement. The downside is, as the area grows, the company may feel compelled to bring in people from the outside to manage it, so you may go from a wearer of many hats and an important part of the operation to just another cog in the machine. At one of my jobs, I actually lost count of how many "leaders" were brought in to manage one specific area I was part of… in hindsight, it was really quite ridiculous. The company had very qualified people in house that could have done the job without all the effort needed to get someone new up to speed. But, as companies can do, they overthought it and wanted someone in charge that had "done it before." This may increase expense, but the company may believe it's worth it because they like the "good optics" associated with having a known name running an exciting new area.

I realize this comes across as somewhat negative, but if given a chance to work in a fast growth or startup area, personally I would always take it, as you never know where opportunity will present itself as the area grows. It may also provide opportunity to advance at an accelerated rate, potentially allowing you to reduce the time it would take waiting for your turn in a stable, slow growth role. The most important thing is to see the opportunity as it is happening and know when to take advantage of it, which is easier said than done.

CHAPTER 29

I Will Be Rewarded for My Loyalty

YOU WILL—AS LONG AS YOU ARE LOYAL TO YOURSELF. THERE IS nothing wrong with showing a level of loyalty to someone who helped you, but loyalty stops when it comes at your own personal detriment or when it stops being a two-way street. At more than one company, I had opportunities to move into new roles working under different leadership in other departments but declined—here's an example of when I did this:

I had a skill set that was pretty broad, especially given my academic business background coupled with my aptitude for understanding technology; both how it works technically, but also how it can be leveraged to benefit the business. I was also a better-than-average analyst and knew my way around spreadsheets and databases, not to mention how to interpret data and turn it into insightful information. A few managers were impressed with my capabilities and offered me roles early in my career. I was flattered, but always turned them down. I was a "team guy" and wanted to stay with whatever my team of the moment was. Looking back, I realize I should have selectively moved to other roles. I was not from a "top tier" school (a silly term some companies embrace that I have learned to loathe) so no one was going to be putting me into any fast-track programs. If I had taken some of those roles, it would have shown that I had an interest in growing and a willingness to take on new challenges. Second, if you are talented, the management of the new team you join is going to feel like they hit the lottery with you. If you impress early, you may be given additional projects or increased responsibility, all opportunities to continue to impress and accelerate your career growth curve. It would have exposed me to additional people, allowing me to learn from others and build out my network that I could leverage in the future... especially if I did good work for them. You never know when you are going to need a reference or recommendation (or a job).

Over time, I learned turning down offers was a mistake on several levels. First, I was usually not the only person in my area looking to grow, so I had competition—and there are only so many promotions to go around. Considering a new area would have cast a wider opportunity net. Second, not all bosses move out of your way. If the person above you isn't moving and doesn't show any interest in moving, you are not going to advance—being loyal in this situation may cost you growth. Additionally, if you are working in an area that is not seen as business-critical to the company, you will not be recognized—even if your work is good and valued by your customers. Loyalty to see something through is a not a poor character trait, but that doesn't mean you have to commit career suicide to prove you are a loyal person. Loyalty isn't bad, but it does need to have its boundaries.

Being overly loyal and sitting around waiting to be recognized was a fool's game. It gave the impression that I was "comfortable," didn't want additional responsibility or to try new things and maybe even gave management the idea that I was happy just coming in, punching the clock and picking up my check. My immediate manager would know better, but that information doesn't always filter its way up the food chain. On top of that, other managers in the group were working hard to make their case for promotions, not resting on the idea that one's work speaks for itself, like I did. I hadn't yet learned, and certainly hadn't mastered politics, so I was at a real disadvantage (though I'm still not sure I mastered politics).

Sometimes, a promotion will occur when someone is good at their job and they put in enough time. That can certainly happen when the environment is conducive for it, but if you are in a career stalling hole, find a way out and take a calculated approach to shaking things up. There is nothing wrong with being loyal but be loyal to yourself first. This may require you be a little selfish when it comes to your career—don't let that deter you, it's OK to want what's best for you. Once you move on, your old position will open up an opportunity for someone else and will be filled… and as difficult as it may be to hear, you may even be quickly forgotten. I didn't have to add the "quickly forgotten" part, but I'm writing about reality, not the fantasy world some people want you to believe exists.

Bottleneck!

I had a few smart bosses. One in particular was very talented, and from my perspective could have moved into other roles. I'm not sure if they were comfortable where they were – perhaps being overly loyal – weren't as highly thought of as I believed, knew they had already advanced to the highest level they could comfortably handle or maybe they were just scared to take on something new. Sometimes additional responsibility comes with additional headaches and drama that they wanted to avoid. Not everyone has the same level of ambition. Maybe there just wasn't as much opportunity for them as I believed. The fact that my boss wasn't moving became more frustrating as I received incremental promotions, eventually being just one level below them… now there is nowhere else to move, at least not up. I was getting greater responsibility, but still in a career hole, I just didn't know it. I should have stopped digging and looked for a way out. This is not a unique scenario; especially at companies that have a deep talent pool. That deep pool makes it difficult for people to continue to advance as talent gets bottlenecked at certain levels. My boss was not to blame, I really don't know why they didn't move, but if this is your situation, you have a decision to make - you can sit and wait for that bottleneck to unwind or you can be proactive and make an independent move. Waiting can work, but it's not a guarantee. Oh, and by the way, I'm pretty sure all the people reporting to me probably didn't understand why I wasn't getting out of their way either.

CHAPTER 30

A Vote of Confidence... Just Not in Me

REMEMBER A SITUATION WHERE AN EXECUTIVE SAW SOMEONE who reported up through me lead a meeting on what is now a long-forgotten topic that I'm sure seemed important at the time. They did a great job. That executive, who had limited background knowledge of this individual, assumed I did not know how to evaluate talent and told my boss to provide this person with more opportunity based on this single encounter.

The executive should have asked me more about the individual and why they presented so well at this meeting yet weren't getting other opportunities, as there were legitimate reasons for this. To be honest, I was relieved when this person was eventually moved to a different area to "impress" but should have realized that the questioning of my ability to manage my team, identify talent, and provide opportunities, meant I was not viewed in a positive way by this executive. My immediate boss was a strong advocate for me, but with little to no knowledge of me personally, this executive had a predefined bias that limited me regardless of my strong performance reviews and supervisor's positive feedback about me. They also had veto power over my boss, so my chances for growth were very limited.

I later found out that I was not alone in how I was being evaluated. Others that reported directly to, or up through this person had similar experiences, and it turns out they only valued people with certain academic and/or vocational backgrounds. Anyone not possessing certain credentials or working in a specific area were seen as less valuable and less capable. It would have been nice to see the person in my example succeed and discover I was wrong about them, but unfortunately, they did not handle the new opportunities provided to them well, and when put in the spotlight, did not deliver. They were let go within a year.

Most of this is on me, as I should have "pushed" this leader to better understand my role. I could have scheduled regular meetings with them, if not monthly, at least quarterly. I should have had them attend my "big" meetings and participate in important decisions I was responsible for to see me in action rather than allow them to make uninformed assumptions about my capabilities. I'm not giving them a free pass, but if someone is judging you without understanding your work, you may need to take the initiative to change that. If they still don't want to engage, then you know it's time to find somewhere or someone that will give you a fair chance.

In hindsight, I probably knew I should have been more engaging with this person, but in the back of my mind I also knew I didn't really connect with them and simply didn't enjoy spending time with them. Every encounter left me drained and feeling bad about myself. Sometimes you need to make something happen—in this instance, the executive in question already had a less than positive opinion of me, so I had nowhere to go but up and engaging with them likely would have been worth the risk. It was a good life lesson that I didn't allow to happen again.

After I left this particular company, I found out the executive was "relieved" of many of their responsibilities and all that remained was an area they previously deemed lesser in value and now had to try to justify the importance of—isn't life funny? It's been years, and I haven't stayed in touch, so I'm not sure how things eventually turned out, but I'm a believer in karma, so my guess is probably not great.

CHAPTER 31

Being in Charge and Being a Leader Are Not the Same Thing

I WORKED WITH A LOT OF SMART EXECUTIVES AND A FAIR NUMBER of them were also really talented leaders. I also worked with some really smart executives who sadly were not talented managers or leaders.

Over the years, I allowed a few "executives" that I didn't respect as leaders to make me feel less than important. If you are made to feel small by someone who is supposed to be a leader of a company, you are in a hole. Stop digging and find a way to get away from them. Being honest with you is fine, especially if it's meant to help you grow. Being mean is unacceptable and it's their shortcoming, not yours.

Here's another thing that can make you feel unimportant. There was one executive who, on more than one occasion, brought in their own people for roles above existing team members that could, and should have been considered for promotions. In some instances, positions were even "created" so they could bring on a friend. There are few things that will frustrate a staff more than this. It is also incredibly frustrating and even demoralizing when you have budget for a much-needed position that could improve the team, just to have that position repurposed for a new and potentially unnecessary role… for a friend of a department head.

Sometimes my job was to train the people who were hired by their executive friend. The problem was, the hires weren't always skilled enough for the role they were being brought in to fill. It's not their fault they were friends with someone who could create a position, but the assumption that an area I worked in was so easy that anyone could do the work was a fallacy. Everyone doesn't just become an analyst, a BA, Project Manager, or an expert in fill-in-the-blank role. LeBron James makes shooting a basketball look easy, but even with what I assume is immense natural talent, it still took him thousands of hours of training and practice to make it look so effortless. Making something look easy doesn't mean it is. For the record, I am not saying I am the LeBron James of my field, it's just an example.

Like me, you may be frustrated by this, but you need to shake it off, as you are going to see it happen—you will. Take the high road and do your best to be helpful and keep contributing.

I'm going to digress a little here again as this made me recall another executive who had "championed" an individual and wanted me to teach them what my team did and how to do it. I did my best, but some people just aren't wired up to be good analytically or with technical details. This doesn't mean they're not smart, it's either not their thing, or the more likely scenario is that it took those doing it years to obtain the knowledge and skills which were not going to be mastered in a couple of weeks. I'm guessing someone could teach me how to weld—I may learn the basics, but even if I was a quick study and was deemed skilled, I sure wouldn't trust my work on a suspension bridge or an airplane after only a few weeks of training. With the luxury of hindsight, it became known that the individuals had a personal relationship and the executive was trying to find a role for that person. When this knowledge was eventually revealed, it was extremely demotivating for everyone else. Team members went to school, obtained degrees, put in years of service, worked and grinded their way through the difficult career paths but what they really should have been working on is building a personal relationship with the boss (this was the prevailing sentiment of the team). Now, anytime someone was overlooked or conversely promoted, everyone wondered if it was for their talent and based on merit, or if they were friends with the boss. What a nightmare!

A High Title Means a Person Can Evaluate Talent

Don't fall into this trap. There were times when I mistakenly equated position title with a broad level of competence. A title may have been earned, but a title alone does not equate to an ability to do all things well.

There were times when I would doubt myself and think I must not be ready for the next step because this particular executive is in a high-ranking position so they must be a good evaluator of talent. They weren't… and not just because they didn't recognize my genius :). In hindsight, I can't think of a single time the individual in this example tried to get to know me or the role I played other than what I assume was a casual glance at an annual performance review. They worked under uninformed assumptions and saw me as little more than a pawn to be sacrificed at will.

At one point in my career, I worked really hard to prove a person's less than positive assessment of me wrong. The good news is, it worked—eventually this executive acknowledged me as a good employee, manager and even leader. You would think I would have felt vindicated, but I didn't—I really just felt stupid for caring what they thought. This is not a person who I respected and I had no reason to prove myself to them. It may have been different if they had a reputation for taking an interest in developing talent, providing honest feedback, being tough-but-fair, but that wasn't the case. Instead, they considered themselves all-knowing and infallible. In hindsight, they simply were not a good leader. Hard lesson to learn, and so much time wasted.

I believe it's just better to move on and find a place where you will be valued. If this person had provided input and feedback on how to grow, develop, or even suggested I find a different path, I may have respected them; rather, they just treated me like an unimportant little cog in a big machine. If you think someone in charge isn't that great of a manager or leader, you may very well be correct. If you think this person is being unfair and will limit your ability to grow and you have options to move, it may be something you want to consider... especially if you are early to mid-way through your career. If you're not careful, you could get stuck here. If you have a small window until retirement, you will need to decide if you can stick it out for a couple of years or if it's bad enough that you have to make a move.

There is No Shortage of Bad Leaders... At Work and at Play

When I played soccer my first year of college, I wasn't the best player on the team, but I knew my role and did my best to make sure I did my part to help the team succeed. There was a time we got lost traveling to a game and had to jump off the bus and onto the field to play or we would have had to forfeit the game—we literally arrived with one minute to spare. We had been driving 10+ hours on the bus and it was hard to just jump straight into the game without warming up. Something broke down early on, and the opposing team scored. I remember coming to the sideline at half-time and one of the coaches berating me for allowing the goal to happen. I tried to tell him that I did what I was coached to do and was sorry there was a breakdown. He needed to blame someone, so he blamed me. Two days later, we watched the film of the game and it was clear I was not at fault. One of our best players made a poor decision resulting in the goal, but the coach didn't apologize or even admit they were wrong. They said nothing—they were not a good coach and not a good leader. The player who made the mistake did speak up and said it was their fault and that I had been wrongly identified as the culprit. They were a good player and a good leader. Work, school, social clubs... whatever the situation, you will encounter bad leaders. I have seen some improve, but not many. Depending on the individual situation, you may or may not be able to get away from them. It's easy to leave a social club or sports collective (not that you should have to, but if you are miserable, you can make this change). It's harder to leave a job, especially if it's a tight market. In the situations where you can't move, continue to focus on being the best you can possibly be while finding ways to improve your skills and develop yourself to be more marketable which can provide a broader set of opportunities for you. This may also be a good time to proactively engage with your network… just in case you need to make an unplanned move.

… When You Become a Leader

When you get that fancy new title, don't start to believe you are as important as you think your title makes you sound. You are important until you're not, and that can happen quickly. Second, unless you're already a jerk, getting a fancy title doesn't mean you need to become one. You can motivate people without acting like a maniac, and I believe people will be more likely to follow you and perform for you if you are kind. Not kind like being a pushover, but kind like you have their best interests in mind. A new title may mean you have to make decisions that are more difficult… things related to budget, staffing (promotions, hiring, firing, etc.) and commitments of resources, to name a few. You may also have more visibility than you've had in the past, but it shouldn't change who you are. Remember, people aren't going to expect you to have all the answers or know everything. They will expect you to do the right things for the company and to hopefully put them in positions to succeed and, if interested, grow and advance. In general I have found that people are smart and capable regardless of their title—treat them like they are.

If there is someone you think is a great leader, you can try to emulate some of that person's traits or even model some of your behaviors to theirs; but keep in mind, everyone is different and emulating someone else may not be a natural fit for you.

If it feels forced, then take what you like about them and find a way to get to the same outcome using your own style and approach. The point here is that you are allowed to be positive and supportive as a boss (or an employee) and can still be effective while being kind. If everyone who has achieved a level of success in the organization you work at is a raving lunatic, you may want to find a path to a different place… or get comfortable working with raving lunatics and understand that in order to advance you, too, may need to become one.

CHAPTER 32

Let's Clean Up

THERE ARE TIMES WHEN PEOPLE ARE BROUGHT IN TO "CLEAN house" and eliminate all the long timers who make good salaries. It may be hard to believe, but I've seen this at more than one company and the few times I've witnessed it, the "house cleaners" also tend to bring in their own people to plug into key positions. One approach is to use intimidation and fear for one's job and to make life so miserable for a person that they simply quit—maybe even saving the company the cost associated with severance.

Often the "cleaners" use what I refer to as positional power—they are in charge, know they are in charge, and leverage their title and role to try to intimidate people to do anything they say. I remember one of these types who found something wrong with everything and would ask questions until they got to one you didn't have an answer for, I guess just to remind you how uninformed you were. On one occasion, after first answering a dozen questions, we got to one that seemed odd and I said "I don't specifically know the answer to that" and their response was "why not, it's knowable." The answer to the Diophantine equation is knowable, too, which I'm sure we would have eventually got to had I kept answering questions correctly. What a turd.

I knew where this was going, so I just bit my tongue and said I would get back with them. I eventually learned how to handle them, but it was always draining. I think an inability to intimidate and control me made this person dislike me – I'm not sure – but whatever the reason, I knew I needed to get away from them. I could have waited it out and tried to win them over, but I've done that before, and had no interest in doing it again. I found a home with a new team and went from being someone to kick around to being highly valued. Being proactive and initiating a move saved this particular job for me.

Another trait I discovered about these people is that they may make disparaging remarks about you to other leaders and try to "talk down" your value to the organization. They think simply saying something somehow makes it true. It's frightening that this can actually work. Not that it will make you feel any better, but it's not personal—just a technique (a chicken-shit one done by weak people, but still). The idea is to talk up their preferred people and believe that by making someone else look bad it makes their preferred people look good (yes, this will really happen). This can be disheartening, as they won't even take two minutes to get to know you and it may be made even worse if you were accustomed to praise and are now being condemned. To have someone who has known you for a short time trying to damage your reputation and potentially your career is terribly frustrating. It is unlikely you are going to win this battle, but you should fight to protect your name and reputation. Some people will try to "wait out" bad managers figuring there will eventually be enough complaints that they will find their way out the door. This becomes less plausible, however, when there are significant changes going on at the organization and waiting out a bad leader may not be an option—especially if they were brought in to do exactly what they are doing. It's likely that they will eventually be gone, as this may be a time-bound role, but don't try to outlast them; you're just going to lose time you could have spent starting a new role in another department or company.

If any of this sounds like your situation, do everything you can to get away from these people—they will suck the lifeforce out of you. I knew a person that went from being on the chopping block to becoming the talk of the town simply by switching positions. They eventually got promoted several times and continued to move into new roles. Their greatest decision was to make a lateral move to get away from a bad boss/leader. In general, bad bosses don't get better, so if you have one, and it looks like they have any staying power, it's probably time to look for a path out.

Saving and investing allows you to be prepared for this exact situation / circumstance. I personally decided a long time ago to never work fearing for my future with any company. I will always give my best, and if that isn't good enough, a company can choose to part ways with me but I definitely won't allow myself to be pushed around. I certainly never want to lose a job, but I won't be bullied, either—I've done that in the past and realized it was an awful way to work and will never do it again. It's always a good feeling knowing you are prepared.

CHAPTER 33

My Role is Mission Critical

THE SAD REALITY IS THAT NO ROLE IS SO CRITICAL THAT YOU can't live without it... well, maybe there is one. I worked at a company where an individual had to "run a job" every night. They were the only one that knew the complicated steps and technical code required and they refused to document it or teach it to anyone else. They were a contractor and worked every day for about 30 minutes but stayed for 8 hours. They didn't even try to hide that they weren't busy. In fact, they literally watched TV the other 7.5 hours of the shift (this is before you could watch TV on your computer or phone, so they had to bring in a portable TV). Interestingly, I should have learned something from this, but didn't... here's a hindsight observation, and although I don't think I'm wired up to do this, I'm going to say it... can't believe I'm going to say it, but I am—here it is: don't teach people your job. I know, I know, you have a fiduciary duty to share information with colleagues if it's good for the company, blah, blah, blah. I believe some of the traditional thinking about this topic is valid and true, and I was always willing to teach anyone anything I knew. But unless you are working in the most progressive company on the planet, once you do this, the person you taught your job to may now want your job and you may now be in their way.

If sharing what you do will save lives, share it. If there are 100 people all doing the exact same job and it's impossible to keep up with the workload, by all means, teach people your job; there are 100 other people that already know how to do it, and you need help. If someone needs help understanding how to do a basic task that would help them, of course teach them. But if you do something unique that differentiates you and makes you marketable and valuable, use discretion in sharing the secret sauce in what you do. This may seem incredibly controversial to some, but there is a reason companies have non-compete clauses with some employees when they leave; one of those reasons being they don't want their competition to know their potentially proprietary processes. As an individual, if you are unique in some way (and possess proprietary skills) you need to leverage that to your own benefit. Half of the people reading this will disagree, but you need to take care of you first.

When there is a clear need to handoff responsibilities/duties to someone so you can take on a new role, it may make sense to teach your job to someone new. If you are just doing it to be a good employee, you may regret it. I can't believe I just wrote that, but people are funny, and even though they may thank you for teaching them something, you may also now be a barrier to their growth. And guess what—they may be cheaper and even better than you and when it comes time to cut some costs, you could be the one who's shown the door. I never personally withheld knowledge, but I've seen it and heard from others that have experienced this.

There was someone I thought wasn't a good employee, and I assumed withheld information out of fear. But there is a part of me that now understands why they did it… and sadly, management may even indirectly incentivize this kind of behavior—here's how. Even though I have learned that there is no role that can't be replaced, companies can sometimes think of an individual (person) as the role. When they do this, they give great power to that person (good for that person). They may get raises or even promoted just to keep them; the company is afraid of what may happen if that person left even though they are unwilling to teach anyone else what they do. It's not preferred behavior, yet it may still be rewarded. I once joked to an officer of a company I worked at that we needed to invest in a Nerf car for an employee because they were so critical to a specific and important process.

One final thought on being mission critical... another way to create some staying power is to take on a job, function or process that no one else wants to do. It may be something that is tedious, less than glamorous, requires interaction with difficult people, etc. Regardless of the reason behind this particular function being deemed undesirable, if you own it, you may find yourself indispensable. If the job is complicated or disinteresting, your boss may never eliminate your role out of fear of having to find someone to back-fill for that task, or even worse, having to take over that work themselves. This is no guarantee, but if the work is important to the company (even though it is not interesting or exciting), it may be a path to longevity, especially if you are good at it.

CHAPTER 34

The Company Wants Me to Succeed

MAYBE. DURING AN EARLY STAGE OF MY PROFESSIONAL CAREER I had made it known that I was interested in taking on more responsibility, and although I was willing to be patient, I wanted to grow. My immediate supervisor was supportive and looked for ways to get me involved in other projects to gain exposure, network, etc. Unfortunately, a more senior decision maker who ultimately had final approval over promotions would find ways to dismiss accomplishments—looking only for negatives and acting as though any creative or improved gain was expected and easy. When nothing is ever good enough, it can be a huge deflator. I continued to stay in this role determined to "prove" I was good, competent and contributed in a way that was worthy of a promotion.

It became known that a role was going to be posted for a new position that was a step up from my current title. The entire team that reported to me, as well as other colleagues, assumed it was being created for me. I had no such knowledge or assumption, but I did expect to be able to apply and hopefully interview for it. One day my boss suggested I watch the job postings for the day as they believed the role was going to be posted, and I should submit my interest. I watched all morning and didn't see anything. After lunch, I watched for the remainder of the day and didn't see anything. I inquired and was told that it had been posted from 12:00—12:30 (during lunch), and it was now closed. I am not making this up.

A few things here:

1 This was a clear message to me that I was not valued... I was in a career hole and should have looked for a way out as quickly as possible.

2 Why even tell me about the role if it's just going to be posted and removed within 30 minutes during lunch? I think it was known that I was interested, but they didn't want me for the role. Basically, I was played. The company totally overthought this and could have just told me they wanted another candidate. I may have asked why, but at least wouldn't have felt like I was manipulated.

3 This same company had less than consistent HR policies and would make exceptions when it suited the company, so in this case it was "sorry, you missed the posting, it's now too late to submit," but I've seen other times when they made exceptions and hired people who hadn't even applied. It really depended on who made the request. I can't imagine the person who was hired just happened to see the posting between 12:00—12:30, it's much more likely they were already the only candidate, but HR needed to "post" the role. This role was filled from the outside but the individual was known by the hiring manager (i.e. a friend). This activity should not have surprised or bothered me, as this (and other forms of favoritism) was a common business practice at this company.

Bonus Takeaway: Never believe HR is there to serve the employee; their job is to protect the company. This isn't necessarily bad; you just need to realize this is a fact. I've seen so many people think HR exists to help employees. I've worked with some talented and very competent HR people and none of them ever "worked" for the employee—they all worked for the company. Always understand this!

Clarification—It's going to sound like every time I applied for something I was turned down, and one could possibly read into this that perhaps I got turned down so often because I wasn't really ready or qualified. The reality is I had consistent progression in every professional job I've held… unfortunately, I also saw a fair amount of rejection (I've been working since I was 16). There could just be a better candidate, and I'm fine if and when that happens, but it's the times when the playing field wasn't level that I'm writing about and the "signs" I should have seen that could have helped me manage my career path more effectively.

CHAPTER 35

Are You Certified?

THIS IS A DIFFICULT TOPIC AS I HAVE A LIKE/HATE RELATIONSHIP with certifications. Certain certifications have garnered broad acceptance and may even be seen as a continuation of a university degree; for example, a Certified Public Accountant (CPA) is a must for anyone with an accounting degree who wants to pursue an upward path in this field. Over the years, other certifications like Six Sigma and LEAN also gained popularity and credibility. I don't know the exact timeline, but even more certifications became readily accepted and desired; for example, in the world of project management. Over time, not just fields but specific industries and even platforms started to have certifications and courses supporting them. Now there are entire industries supporting certifications for platform(s) from training to mock tests and prep courses. I'm not sure where the line should be drawn, but some of these offerings are truly certifications while others are just completing XYZ hours of coursework… at best, to stay current; at worst just to say you are certified while these prep companies ring the cash register.

One platform I'm familiar with has 20+ certifications you can obtain. These certifications many times also require renewals, which just keeps the supporting industry churning. When looking for a job candidate, is hiring someone with 19 certifications better than hiring someone with 18? I guess if the 1 that differentiates them is the one that your company focuses on or needs it may benefit them, but if that's the case, then 1 would also be better than 18 (assuming the 18 are missing the critical 1). It's really become a bit watered down, at least in my opinion. What happens when a company hires the one with 18 instead of 19? Are they opening themselves up to a lawsuit? When a company asks for qualifications, are they asking for specific certifications, or generically "certified"? Does obtaining a 4-year degree or a Master's count for anything any longer, or is it all about the certifications?

There are certain certifications I could obtain in my fields—some require X hours or X years of experience before becoming eligible for a test, but it always seemed silly to me to take a test to prove I can do the job I've been doing for years... especially when some of the "certified" people I've worked with really weren't very good at a job they were supposedly certified to do. Sure, they have a base level of knowledge, know some technical aspects, and have a collection of letters or acronyms after their title, but lack experience implementing, managing or leading anything in the real world. I knew one friend whose company certified them in a day just to say they were certified while bidding on a job. Is that legitimate? I don't know the answer to that question, because they were absolutely competent in their field; all the certification did was satisfy some company's credential requirement for a role.

At the time of this writing, certifications seem to be important to many organizations as well as to the industries that promote them. So, although it sounds like I'm anti-certification, I'm going to suggest if you have a chance to obtain them in your field, definitely take advantage of the opportunity; especially if an employer is willing to pay for it. Working on a certification can also put some purpose back into a job that may have become routine and reinvigorate your interest in developing your skills. Working on a certification may also expand your network with new people, which can certainly be helpful.

I experienced some minor challenges not having taken some of these tests and obtaining said certifications—in addition to what I've already mentioned, they can also help differentiate you and make you more marketable, put you on par with your competition and take away an excuse not to hire or promote you (or potentially give you a poor performance review for not being certified).

I believe there is a place for certifications—I even have a few—but I also think some fields and products are over certified and need to be reined in. Just being curious here, but I wonder how many certifications the likes of Bezos, Gates and Musk each have. If only a few or none, imagine how successful they may have become if they had 20!

CHAPTER 36

Who Am I?

Don't Lose Your Identity

I CAN'T TELL YOU THE NUMBER OF TIMES I'VE TOLD MY WIFE HOW disappointed I was in myself for allowing more than one role I've held define who I was. There was part of me that liked answering the "what do you do" question, because many times, what I did was complicated and, from my point of view, important work. I had an "executive" title, had multiple teams reporting to me and I managed millions of dollars in projects and assets. I hated that "what do you do" morphed into who I was. Answering emails or texts after hours, on weekends and while on vacation became a badge of honor. Joking how PTO (planned time off) was really "pretend" time off. Losing vacation days at the end of the year because I was just too busy to take them. All things I now look back at and cringe. Hopefully you will learn sooner than I did on how to separate work from personal. That doesn't mean if an important project is happening that you should wash your hands of responsibility, but it shouldn't be a 365 days per year practice or expectation.

I totally understand how hard this is to do; especially early in your career. Someone right out of college may go from making $20-$30K/ year (or nothing) to $80-$100K or more and it feels great. When you have a limited income, you learn the value of money and once you start having disposable income you never want to lose the buying power that income affords you. To make it even more difficult, if you work even harder, you can potentially make even more money. It's a never-ending spiral and there are definitely roles where time devoted to a job has a direct correlation to an ability to advance and earn more. Here's the deal—some jobs may require more commitment than others, and you should definitely do whatever is needed to provide for your family, but I would urge you to find a way to keep your identity independent from your work—otherwise, when you leave work in 20+ years, or lose your job, you will have also lost your identity.

My real identity is being available for my family, involved in the community, looking for ways to create solutions that help people and animals and to provide insight, guidance and assistance to those who need it… from a business or personal perspective. I do these things because it's who I am, what I am and what I do.

… And Be Authentic

You hear this term a lot now, and if you look up what it means you'll find many different interpretations. People being authentic has been happening long before it was a buzz phrase. To me, it means being comfortable in your own skin, sticking to your convictions and following your heart—not the latest fad. I had a manager who really embraced this and encouraged people to be OK with who they were and to accept others' differences. Keep in mind, it's a work environment and you still have to adhere to certain professional standards and expectations, so if your authentic self prefers to not bathe or wear deodorant, it may be an issue… just like if your authentic self is belittling, mean or likes to say inappropriate comments. If that describes you, don't be authentic. Knowing your leadership is supportive of an approach that embraces authenticity provides some comfort to know you are allowed to be true to yourself without the concern of judgement.

Here's the rub—this worked great with most of the team, but if the rest of the organization doesn't embrace this philosophy, it can cause problems. Employees in other areas may find it ridiculous, or they may find it refreshing and desirable—either way, it can cause friction because it's something they don't have. The same is true for leaders in other areas. You may even have some team members who find it inappropriate—there are some that see work as... well, work. It should not be a place where you are allowed to be yourself; they think you should be whatever the company wants you to be since the company is paying you. This isn't my stance, but I have definitely seen it.

Brace yourself; not everyone is going to like authentic you—if the person who doesn't like the authentic you is also the person who approves raises and promotions, then you may need to find a happy medium between authentic you and the you who can work well with that person. For example, the way I deal with stress is to use humor... not mean or inappropriate humor, more self-effacing and observational, but not everyone welcomes this. One of my former bosses was born without a funny bone and saw no humor in anything. I'm not sure if their family was once harmed by a comedian, but they really had no interest in anything other than staying in a straight and narrow lane and never deviating. I'm guessing it worked for them and helped them get to where they were, so they saw no reason to change. When you are confronted with situations like this, you will need to adjust. You don't need to change who you are, but you do need to be self-aware enough when talking with those who don't like anything outside their comfort zone to pivot... and by the way, you are not going to change them, so don't waste any time trying.

The other thing I think about when discussing being authentic is the need to follow your moral compass. In other words, don't do something just because everyone else is doing it or simply because you were told to do it. If you are an honest person by nature, and you are asked to alter results or cheat on an expense report, it's going to go against your own internal values. Here's the simple answer... don't do it.

More Authentic Talk... Well, Kind Of—People are able to get to the same solution using different approaches. I've learned doing it "my way" can be just as effective as doing it "your way." It took me a while to embrace this, but it's OK; in fact "different" can be valuable and assures you've covered a broad range of possibilities and considered multiple options. This is a little bit of a stretch, but a group of co-workers met for lunch one day and after we arrived and were seated, I asked everyone what route they took to arrive at the restaurant and why they took that route. There were basically 4 routes people took, and the reasons they took them were based on the following: the fastest, the safest, the least construction and it was the way they knew. All made perfect sense, and I understood each approach. The person who said it was the way they knew asked others about their routes and now had other options for the future. We all ended up at the same destination, and if there had been some urgency, more may have taken the quickest route, or opted for GPS assistance, but with no need to take any risk some opted for a safer approach. The parallels to work are pretty obvious here, but I like food so I decided to throw in a restaurant experience.

Here's what I know for sure about being authentic: if you hate going to work every day because you have to be or act like someone you are not, that unhappiness can seep into your non-work life. If you are comfortable going to work and enjoy what you do, that happiness can also carry over to your non-work life. For those with a great home life, neither scenario will likely move the needle much at the house, but for those with challenging home lives, a great job can offer a distraction and some normalcy from a challenging home life and maybe make the day bearable. A lousy job coupled with a challenging home life is not a good recipe.

If being authentic helps you enjoy work, then be as authentic as the culture you work in allows. My simple advice for a good work/life balanced relationship is… when possible, try to enjoy what you do.

CHAPTER 37

You Won a Major Award!

L ET ME START BY SAYING: I'VE NEVER BEEN TERRIBLY IMPRESSED by awards—I actually find them to be a little silly, especially the ones that have no tangible criteria used to identify the "winner." One of my first experiences with corporate "awards" was when I attended a celebratory company event with a friend—I was a college student and the grand prize was about to be drawn on stage. The prize was $10,000! I thought, holy cow, if I could win this, it would change my life. I was a broke college student who wasn't even sure I could make rent that month. For a brief second, I thought life was fair and I may actually have a chance… I quickly calculated that there were about 1,000 people in the room, and company employees were not eligible, so my odds, although not great, were definitely better than the lottery (my friend worked for the company, I didn't). Right before the drawing, my friend leaned over and told me who was going to win… and then they did. I said, "how did you do that," and they told me "oh, that's our biggest client, our biggest client always wins." This was too funny, and it basically was nothing more than a $10K bribe to keep the decision-maker happy and assure continued business for the upcoming year, which was worth millions. This was a private company conducting this drawing, and I'm pretty sure what they did wasn't illegal (but I don't really know what limitations this particular industry has on "buying" business, so maybe it was)… legal or not, at a minimum is felt unethical.

One company I worked at loved awards. If they needed to, they would make up categories to assure a new or old or fill in the blank client won one. As part of my training with this company, I had an opportunity to do a road trip with some of our customer facing employees and while waiting to meet with a customer, the person I was shadowing showed me some of the awards the company I worked for gave this customer—they were proudly displayed in a trophy case in the lobby. It was shared that they were all made up and that they just create any award to keep them happy. This didn't completely shock me, but I found the casual nature in telling me how fake they all were surprising. I've also been part of committees to evaluate criteria and determine a given award's winner(s). Sadly, when you pull the curtain back you quickly realize that the criteria would change to make sure the award found its way into the desired hands. Any calculated criteria were weighted; I would estimate 1% tangible criteria, 99% whatever the company wanted—OK, not quite that slanted, but not exactly unbiased.

If someone wins an award instead of you, don't get too discouraged—especially if it was a popularity contest instead of based on well-defined criteria (although I guess you could worry a little if it was a popularity contest and this was some sort of validation that you are not popular… sorry). If you win an award instead of someone else, don't get too excited, it may have just been your turn. I'm not saying all awards are fake or even bad, but have your eyes fully open and your brain fully informed when someone gets one—it's not always as big of a deal as you would believe. By the way, I've seen award recipients be fired not long after receiving them, so they're not some talisman that guarantees a job.

I have an outdoor area on the side of my house that won't grow any vegetation; it has something to do with the way the sun hits or doesn't hit it. I filled that area with stone, so it isn't a mud pit. Along with the stone, I also relocated most of my Lucite and metal awards and mixed them in with the stone in the same area. At the end of the day, do good work because that's what you are supposed to do, not to get an award. Now, if an award happens to be a way to get promoted and make more money, and if that is important to you, then by all means, try to get that award.

CHAPTER 38

I'm Newsworthy

YOU WILL SEE PUBLICATIONS THAT RECOGNIZE YOUR COMPANY IN a featured article, and you may think… wow, the company must be doing some really special work to receive such recognition. It may even be a feature story about an individual at the company who gets acknowledged for some forward-thinking, industry specific approach or some hype about their unparalleled leadership. It could be an actual publication that does such features, but it could also be nothing more than a PR campaign. Some companies partially or fully fund industry publications or they buy so much advertising in them that they may as well be funding them… so, of course the "publication" is going to feature very pro-company stories. The company may need copy points about an individual, so they basically create them through some "feature" article in a magazine.

This becomes very obvious when you start your own business. I can't tell you how many "magazines" and "publications" have offered to do stories about my business… for a fee, of course. I've actually considered using this approach just to see if it works but even though it's an accepted practice, it just doesn't feel right to me. I may get worn down and still do it, but I think I prefer a brighter line defining the difference between journalism and sponsored content than what this is.

Not every feature piece is manufactured; some companies and some individuals have earned the recognition that gets highlighted by an "article." Definitely don't turn down an opportunity to be featured; I'm sure it's awesome to have nice things written about you, but as the saying goes, don't start believing your own press. Having something nice said about you doesn't give you a free pass to anything, you still have to deliver on your commitments like everyone else.

Also, a lot of people may not really care that you had anything "written" about you. If you have a nice feature done on you, enjoy it, but don't let it go to your head. And for those glowing company stories you read, just remember they may have been written or (possibly) influenced by the company. I tend to follow the old Poe quote, which reads: "Believe half of what you see and nothing of what you hear".

CHAPTER 39

Glad I Interviewed For That...?

ONE OF MY JOB INTERVIEWS WAS FOR AN INTERNAL ROLE THAT would have been a step up for me and was in an area that I was highly qualified for. Even though one of the people on the interview panel had a personal relationship with one of the other candidates, I still thought I had a pretty good chance. I was delivering good work, helping the area I currently worked in grow, had proven myself as a good manager, team builder and developer of people and had relationships with other organizations that would be working with this new position. I wouldn't have been surprised if I got the role; after all, I was qualified for it. I also wouldn't have been surprised if it was offered to another qualified person who also had a little bit of an inside connection with one of the interviewers.

What did surprise everyone was when the role was extended to someone who didn't interview and wasn't even part of the conversation. It is possible that all the candidates, including me, simply underwhelmed in the interviews and they needed to look elsewhere, but at least they could have tried to conceal the sham by requiring the person who ultimately got the role to go through the same process as everyone else. The person selected was smart and capable and ended up doing fine, but it was a real punch to the gut for those of us who worked hard to prepare. The person hired was from within the department head's team structure, and they just decided to promote them. This is fine, but why waste everyone's time with this farce?

A few people said things like "at least going through the process was a good experience, and it let everyone know you are interested in growing." I guess this is somewhat true, but I wasn't really looking for a silver lining—either way I didn't get the promotion, and to be honest I wasn't going to be any happier if the person who did get it had actually interviewed. The part that ticked me off was having to waste my time. Here's what's interesting… and I guess ironic (if I'm using that correctly)—most of my promotions came the same way; I never had to interview for them. I'm sure there was probably some person just like me wondering why they were put through the hassle of interviewing. Now that person's boss is aware they are looking to leave, which I guess could help them leverage a promotion if they are valued or it could just put a target on them. The reality is, the hiring manager usually knows who they want and they post the position, and in some cases even interview, because they have to follow a set of HR rules or possibly even laws. This is reality, and you are going to experience this. Life isn't fair, and you shouldn't expect it to be. Do your best when provided an opportunity; you never know where it will lead—just don't spend any of that new salary before you actually get the job.

Speaking of interviews, I used to get pulled into being part of the "interview panel" for other managers and leaders that were hiring people. It was a big production with specific documents to fill out—a designed methodology using a catchy acronym for asking questions (make sure they are the same for everyone so everyone can be fairly and equally assessed). There was an HR representative leading the effort and a big meeting after all the candidates had been interviewed to discuss the strengths and weaknesses of each. In one of these examples, the absolute least prepared and seemingly least qualified person was eventually awarded the role. I asked the hiring manager about their decision and was told that they already knew who they were going to hire, and they just had to follow the HR process. Suffice it to say, I rejected any future invitations to participate in these sessions—such a waste of time for this mockery.

Here's the takeaway... you need to have good relationships and a good network. Although there is a component of what you know, WHO you know is always extremely important. Being good is important, too, but there are a lot of talented people, and quite frankly many of them can probably do whatever job it is you are applying for. The best way to get the role is to know someone on the inside, or even better, the hiring manager. I'm not saying this is always true or the only way, but it certainly doesn't hurt. Many job postings are simply posted to satisfy some requirement. Many interviews are conducted to satisfy some requirement. Definitely give yourself better odds by knowing the person who is hiring or someone on the inside. Let me say it one more time—who you know is important.

The other takeaway... people will try to waste your time. Do your best to avoid time-wasting activities; you will never get that time back... and for goodness sake, don't waste other people's time, either. I can assure you they have enough on their plate to keep them busy without you adding something else.

CHAPTER 40

Wombats! Not Specifically a Work Story, But You'll See the Connection

THINK THE SAYING "IT'S NOT THE DESTINATION, IT'S THE JOURNEY" is credited to Ralph Waldo Emerson, although there is some debate. This is not about the origins of the saying or the specific meaning it's believed he was going for, rather it's an internal debate about if the saying really has merit. I'm sure there are thousands of articles and books about "the journey" vs "the destination" and I am definitely not the first to ponder the concept.

I do subscribe to this belief in some cases, as there are times in our lives this makes a lot of sense. The journey while dating your spouse and eventually living with them (hopefully happily) and going through all the fun and crazy experiences that shape us into who we become (the journey) as a married couple (the destination) can be wonderful. I don't have kids, but I'm sure there is something similar parents experience watching their children be born, go to school, graduate, get married, have a family, etc.

Here's one of my journey stories…

The Great Ocean Road! I remember a trip I took with my wife to Australia. We had purchased tickets for a dinner on a streetcar (or railcar, something like that). It seemed a little touristy, but received good reviews, and we had to eat so why not make it interesting. We had the entire day to fill, so we started to drive on something called The Great Ocean Road. In hindsight, how this wasn't on our radar is a mystery, but we knew nothing about it. We calculated how far out we could go before we would have to turn around and make it back for dinner. It was a little rainy and seemed like it was going to be a miserable day, but it had to be better than just sitting in the hotel room. As luck would have it, the sky cleared up and it turned out to be a beautiful day. By the time we got to our "turn around" point we both looked at each other and agreed there was no way we were turning back. I guess I should have mentioned that we are both big nature lovers and prefer a view of trees or the ocean to a city skyline, so if you hate nature, this is your chance to bail out of this chapter.

We "forfeited" our seats and the cost of dinner on the railcar (or whatever it was) back in the city and just kept driving. Google maps may have existed, but my phone at the time had no such thing, so we navigated off of a map located on the back of some tourist informational handout. We went for hours and hours, stopping along the way just to look at the same ocean from a different point of view again and again. We explored little towns, ate at restaurants we just stumbled upon, watched the tide roll in (and almost got stuck in a cave as it came up...) saw where a river literally met the ocean and simultaneously had one foot in each. We walked through a forest and saw wildlife up close and personal. At times, we were the only two people on the planet exploring some of this beautiful scenery. We finished the day off by finding a tiny town with one open restaurant and had the best fish dinner we can remember ever having. During dinner, we talked about how great the day was and how lucky we were to experience what we had just experienced all because we didn't worry about the pre-paid dinner back in the city.

We thought the day was over and now had a many- hours ride back from where we came. So, we topped off the tank and started on our way. We saw, on the less than detailed map, that there was a "shortcut" of sorts back to where we needed to go, so we threw caution to the wind and took it. I wouldn't see the sky the way we saw it this night again until we visited Yosemite during a meteor shower years later. It was unspoiled by any city lights and everything was visible, bright and really just amazing to look at. It's cliché, but boy does it make you feel small. Again, we couldn't believe our great fortune for a clear night and a highway where we only saw other cars every 30 minutes or so. There were a few times we wondered if we were on the right track, because it was desolate with very few landmarks, but finally we saw a familiar city name and knew we were on the right path. I don't really remember getting back to the hotel or falling asleep that night, but I do remember this wonderful detour that stays with me today.

…And Sometimes the Journey Isn't As Fun:

The journey to get to the destination (where we also had a journey—oh that's deep…anyway) started in Dallas, went to Los Angeles with a 5-hour layover, then on to Australia. Brutal, pure and simple—it felt like we were being punished for a crime we didn't know we committed.. Our flight back was even worse; we arrived at the airport in Sydney, made it through security and at the time there was a volcano erupting in Italy that somehow affected our flight. We were told there was an 8-hour delay, which we had to wait out in a sparsely appointed gate that had a few seats, a concrete floor and a soda machine. Thank goodness we packed some snacks. We were exhausted before getting on the plane back to LA, where we would have another 5-hour layover, then on to Dallas. Oh, and the video screen at my seat on the plane was broken, so for 13+ hours I had no entertainment and because it was a full flight, I couldn't move. When we arrived in LA, I remember being a walking zombie and almost bumped into an airport worker—he took terrible offense and asked me if I had a problem… his co-workers were standing around laughing. Wow, I never thought being tired would potentially get me roughed up by an airport employee. Welcome home! We still had to kill five hours, then take a 3ish hour flight back to Dallas. A quick deviation here: anyone who thinks you should dress fashionably instead of comfortably for air travel has clearly never done this trip. We finally got back to Dallas and jokingly said, "I hope our car starts…" I quickly realized that I should not have tempted fate by saying this, but thankfully fate wasn't listening, and it started. There is no part of this "journey" that had any redeeming qualities—it just sucked. Although the journey was terrible, without it we never would have experienced our destinations.

You really don't know which journey is going to be amazing or possibly lead to something amazing… sometimes you have to throw caution to the wind and embark on one. They're not always going to be great, but I've learned they can be worth the risk.

CHAPTER 41

Money Talk

WHO SAYS MONEY ISN'T IMPORTANT... PEOPLE WHO HAVE money. It's easy to say that money isn't important, especially once you have, and no longer need to worry about having it. For the record, money is important, as it buys security for you and your family. It pays for food, shelter, clothing, healthcare, education, transportation, vacation... you name it. And the more money you have, the less stressed you will be about the things that have a cost. People with millions of extra dollars in the bank will say money isn't important but they are living with the security blanket of money around them. If you suddenly took away a very wealthy person's money and they no longer had the comfort knowing it was there if they needed it, I wonder if they would still believe this.

Know Your Value—If you struggle to make rent or pay your mortgage every month, money is likely important to you and can be a real motivator. There have been times when I thought I should have received raises, been promoted, or awarded bonuses... not because I wanted them (which I did) but because I believe I earned them. I didn't expect a promotion every year or the highest raise possible annually, but when you see others around you not contributing the same way but getting recognized due to personal relationships, you begin to have an issue. I shouldn't complain; I made what many would consider a good salary most of my career, but I likened it to a baseball player hitting .350 (if you don't know baseball, that's good) and getting paid less than someone sitting next to them hitting .175 (if you don't know baseball, that's bad). I would do my best to articulate the value I brought to a company and explain why I believed I was worth the investment. Sometimes this would work, other times it fell on deaf ears. Point being: if you find you are contributing at a high level, but your value is not being recognized with higher compensation, it may be time to look for a place that will value you.

The agreement with every company I worked for is this: do good work and get paid an agreed upon amount. However, when a company puts incentive programs in place that would allow you to earn more money by meeting certain criteria, the equation changes a little. The new assumption is: do great work, get paid even more. This does happen, but not always. If you are being recognized and compensated for your contributions, terrific—if not, it may be time to find a place that will compensate you in a way that is commensurate with your contributions. The window for earning a good salary will not stay open forever—you need to take advantage of it while you can.

I'll Work For Free—I do think you should always do good work, but looking back at my career, I would never work as hard as I did during my time off (including evenings, weekends and while on vacation). All this did was create the expectation that I would always be available. When a less dedicated employee would occasionally step up, they would look great and be celebrated because they typically never work on weekends or after hours, so when they did, they got recognized and rewarded. Conversely, if you always work extra hours and you now choose not to, you may be looked upon as disappointing. If you can pull it off, try to only work during work hours and only be available after hours when critically important.

If you say you will be available all the time, there will be an expectation that you actually are available all the time. You may work in a culture that rewards this; if that is the case and if you are comfortable with it and want to grow, then go for it. However, if you are not going to be rewarded for it, don't do it, or it will become a permanent expectation. If the culture at your company expects extra and/or after-hours work, you better learn to either be OK with it or look for something different. Life is short, and there are probably more important and interesting things to do than work 24/7.

CHAPTER 42

Somebody Save Me!

THIS SECTION IS ABOUT SIMPLE MATH. TAKE ADVANTAGE OF 401K matching; it's free money. Take advantage of buying stock at a discount; it's free money. Save, then save some more!

Buckle in, it's a car story. I have a 15 year old truck. I paid it off in 3 years, so I have not had a vehicle payment in 12 years. Let's assume the average monthly vehicle payment is $465 The number doesn't need to be exact, the financial lesson is going to be the same. That means by not having a car payment for the past 12 years (144 months) I have saved $5,580 annually or $66,960 over that 12-year period. Imagine what could you have done with all that additional disposable income!

Let's now assume instead of just repurposing that money as disposable income, that I invested it…I could do the calculation that shows an annual return of X% per year over that period of time, but I'm a stock investor, so let's pick some big and well- known names that have been around for 12 years. For simplicity, I am factoring in dividend reinvestment. Also for simplicity, I am going to assume I invested the annual savings amount every year on first trading day in January. So every January 2 (or first trading day), I invest $5,580 in a stock (I did a lump sum instead of showing monthly…the numbers will change over time, depending on the stock I invested in, but for the most part I'm going to come out way ahead).

The stocks I picked were Microsoft, Apple and Amazon. In 2008, when I paid my truck off, Microsoft was a household name, Apple was 6 months removed from introducing the iPhone and Amazon was continuing to grow its online presence and was a well-established brand with consumers.

I'm not going to do the math, because stock prices change by the minute, but look up any of those (or other well-known names) and do the same calculation. I can almost guarantee you are going to show a huge return. The last time I ran the numbers, it showed the $66,960 I saved over those 12 years would be worth somewhere between $400K and $850K. That number will vary based on investment, but even if it's cut in half, it's still impressive.

I did some of what I describe above, and although I wasn't disciplined enough to invest the entire amount, my wife and I did have an ability to travel and do some things we would not have otherwise been able to do had we spent all that money on a new car every time our old car was paid off. My passport has over a dozen stamps in it because I chose to drive the same vehicle for longer than most people do. Instead of travelling, I could have paid off our house in 12 years, but we like to travel and that's a trade-off we were willing to make.

If your bank account is full of money and you have more disposable income than you know what to do with, enjoy that new car! If that is not your scenario, and you want to alter your future and grow your savings, you may want to consider a reliable vehicle that you keep for a while, and invest what would have been payments – future you will appreciate it. I guess I need to say this, because someone is going to misinterpret what I just wrote…so, for the record, this is an individual decision, and I am not recommending any stock or a specific approach to investing… I'm just sharing my opinion and what works for me.

CHAPTER 43

The Company Loves Me;
I'm Going to Work Here Forever

BEEN THERE, DONE THAT... SEVERAL TIMES. THE COMPANY MAY indeed love you. You are good at what you do, you are dedicated, you embody their real, or at least published values, you fit the culture and are a team player. They may even reward your talents with a great salary... until they don't. Companies are funny; one year they are doing great or their culture is people first, maybe they have generous perks and offer flexible time off, along with other great benefits... then they don't. You need to understand that things can change and change quickly.

The economy may change, competition may enter the market, investments may dry up, there may be a merger, buyout/takeover, economic conditions are altered, government regulations may change, new leaders move away from a people first culture to a financial first one... you may be good, but too expensive for what you do. As the company grows, new, younger and cheaper resources may be able to do what you do, or automation puts you out of work. I'm not trying to paint a grim picture, but don't ever get too comfortable, as change can and will happen.

Reorganizations are another category of change. I worked at a couple of places that had annual (or more) reorganizations. There are different reasons these happen—here are a few:

- New leaders come in and want things a certain way, so they change a team, department or maybe even the entire company.

- I've known some leaders who reorganize so it appears that they are adding value—they think changing things makes them look visionary or important. In some cases, there really was no need for any change, but changing keeps people busy. It's pretty rare to have anyone go back to compare post-reorg results with pre-re-org measurements to determine if the change was effective and impactful.

- A position is created for a new person. Responsibilities are div-vied up and people moved around to support the new role.

- Trying to copy a competitor. Some companies are never on the forefront; rather, they copy others that seem to be doing things differently, maybe better. The irony here is by the time the copycat decides to copy, things may already be changing again—especially if the one that led the way with the initial change discovered it was the wrong approach. Now, the imitator is implementing a bad solution and is behind the curve again.

Some reorganizations make total sense. For example, if multiple functional areas are hiring similar resources to do similar roles, it may make sense to consolidate those roles into a centralized pool of talent that implements standards across the board. I have personal experience where multiple areas were independently creating analytical teams to generate reporting, provide tracking and operational support for various areas. It made more sense to combine those resources and leverage efficiency of a similar talent pool and have all adhere to a consistent set of standards.

...or if two or more companies come together, it's going to be nec-essary to combine teams/resources and figure out the correct structure to support the new company.

There are even times when reorganizations are done as a way to cut costs (I know it's hard to believe). It's also a convenient way to eliminate jobs without having to jump through extra hoops that Human Resources may require. Simply eliminate the role of the person you want to send packing and put the new structure in place. People may threaten to sue, but they rarely do—it can be expensive, may make them un-hirable in the future and companies have done this enough to know how to stay within protective legal boundaries. At more than one company, I've seen many "eliminated positions" simply retitled and given to someone new, or all the work associated with the eliminated position given to someone different, but with a lower title and salary. I once had the great pleasure of keeping my old job while also taking on another, incrementally new, department to manage. That department was previously managed by a person with a higher title than me and now I was responsible for both it and my old job, with a lower title and no promotion... yay, corporate America! I actually welcomed this change and took the new role on with a smile... I saw it as a vote of confidence in my ability. In reality, it was probably more related to cost savings for the company, but I'm going to keep believing it was a nod to my impressive managerial and leadership skills. Companies are in business to make money, not to help people succeed—sorry if I ruined that secret for you. I was going to share something about the Easter Bunny, but maybe I should hold off given the previous bombshell you just read.

In the preceding section, I said companies are funny—well people are funny, too. When things are going well and everyone is happy it feels like the ride will never end—don't believe it; at some point it can end. New leaders will come into a company and may bring their own people with them, have a specific way they want to configure an area, may have been asked to implement the flavor of the month structure that you no longer fit, may be a terrible manager, may not like you for any number of reasons, including seeing you as a threat. For whatever reason, things can change quickly and you need to be ready to protect yourself. I've also seen very supportive managers turn on people when it becomes a numbers game. If it's either them or you that needs to go, I can assure you they are working to make sure it's not them. If your inner voice is telling you something seems off, something is probably off.

One employer I worked for tended to reorganize frequently and after each one I used to come home and tell my wife "I got another 6-month extension on my contract." There wasn't really a contract, but it had that feel to it because of this practice. I never truly felt like an employee there, as the sword of Damocles was always hanging over me, knowing the next organizational change was only 6-12 months away. This is not a healthy way to work or live, but it is reality for many—so, you need to work on having the mindset that you could be without a job at any moment, even if you are good at what you do. Stay engaged with your network and be "ready" if the worst happens.

You can usually tell when things are feeling different—if your spidey sense is telling you something, listen to it. If you don't know what the spidey sense reference means, it's related to the superhero Spiderman who had an extra sense for when something was amiss… but you don't have to be a superhero to have one.

Speaking of Protecting Yourself

I was responsible for managing a vendor relationship and they were trying to sell the company expanded services. First, there was no budget for the services; second, we didn't need the services and third, this vendor practiced a one-way relationship… whatever was good for them, not the customer. It was the end of their fiscal year, and when I told them I wasn't going to buy anything else from them they called my boss' boss and told them how poorly I was managing the relationship and how I was doing a disservice to my company and costing them money. My boss' boss rarely spent any time with peons like me, so they didn't know me that well –although if life was fair, my work should have spoken for itself and they should have understood my approach was always doing what was in the best interest of the company. Instead, they lashed out at my boss and asked what I was doing. The good news is, I'm pretty analytical in nature and had put together a spreadsheet showing our usage of this vendor's product, our need for the next 2 years, the cost associated with buying additional services (that we didn't need) and the savings we could achieve by changing some of the ways we leveraged their product. My boss already knew I would have done this analysis and defended me (a good boss). They then took my analysis to their boss (my boss' boss) and showed them the reasoning behind my decision. My boss also reached out to the vendor that tried to throw me under the bus and reiterated my role and that I was their contact, not two levels above me. I was safe, but it didn't stop these fools from doing this again and again. This continued to happen because they would rotate reps every few months and they were all using the same playbook on how to "sell" to their clients. They didn't care about potentially ruining my career at this company; they were just trying to make additional commissions.

Fortunately, I knew how this organization operated and protected myself from unwarranted backlash, but not everyone is as lucky. I wonder how many other people these jerks got in trouble who weren't prepared with data to back up their decisions. Sadly, this aggressive approach probably works since they seem to have embraced it. By the way, shame on my boss' boss for listening to the opinion of an outsider who got paid by selling the company more stuff over the opinion of someone who had a fiduciary duty to the company (me). The phrase "no good deed goes unpunished" comes to mind. Always be mindful of who you are dealing with, and I personally follow the philosophy of "data doesn't lie." Not every decision can be made analytically, but where you can utilize analysis to help arrive at a decision or validate it, do so. No one can argue with facts (OK, anyone can argue with anything —but data and facts help).

CHAPTER 44

You're a Valuable Part of the Company, Kind Of...

I DIDN'T KNOW IT AT THE TIME, BUT THE DEPARTMENT I WAS working in was not seen as a critically important area. I knew what we did, and the tremendous value we provided, but none of that mattered as management didn't see the department as mission critical. The area was very operational in nature—I used to refer to it as the engine under the hood... no one saw it, but if it wasn't running, the department (maybe the company) wouldn't run, either. I'm sure other departments were the wheels, the brakes, the gas, maybe the radio – I don't know – but I knew we were an integral part of the vehicle. Unfortunately, depending on the company, there may be a bias about which areas are important or critical. It also depends on who you report up to at the executive level. If they came from the technical side or the marketing side or the sales side, it will have an impact.

That history may determine how much they plan to invest in the area, and ultimately its people. Unfortunately, that was my situation. I had one department report to me that just about every other department in the company depended on, but it was also viewed as the weird cousin of departments. People's inability to understand it's confusing complexities (for various legitimate reasons) made it viewed as a barrier instead of as an enabler. People would work twice as hard to go around an established process, in some cases required by law, than just follow it... and because you either manage the department or work in it, you unfortunately become guilty by association. Some of this is on me, as I should have done a better job educating the company on our value, but I like to think I did the best I could with the resources I was provided. Even if this department was "the engine," it was out of sight, out of mind, and if the hood was ever up it was just seen as a jumble of wires and parts that was hard to understand. I was deep in a career hole, and although I've never been one to run away from a challenge, this area simply wasn't valued, meaning no matter how good of a job I did, I would never be seen as valued, either.

These are generalizations, but if you work at a technology company, they're probably going to put high value on developers, not the accounting department; an advertising company may not care about HR, and a clinical company may have little regard for operations or support. All companies are not this way, but I've seen and heard about enough examples to know certain companies have their biases, and those biases can translate into barriers for individual growth.

There are multiple takeaways here:

Life isn't fair, don't ever expect it to be. Just assume this is always a takeaway.

If you know the department you work in is not seen in a favorable way, you are definitely in a career-limiting hole. Open your eyes and realize investment in the department, including you, is unlikely. You may want to consider looking at which departments are in favor and try to find a way to create a career path in one of those areas. I've seen people feel like they can't move even though they may be in a dead-end job with limited upward mobility. I think this is mostly out of fear or maybe they are great at what they are doing and don't want to learn something new. The reality is, if the area is not seen as important and valuable, and you want to grow within the company, you need to get out of that area.

If your skills and contributions, assuming they are legitimate, are not being recognized, you are in a career hole. Find a department or company that will acknowledge what you bring to the table. I realize this is not always possible—you may have limited options where you live, the company may pay well and you can't match that pay somewhere else, you may have dependents that require stability, have a very specialized skill that is not seen as transferrable; there can be many challenges. If you have to stay, try to find a way to tolerate and make the best of the situation but also continue to work on making yourself as marketable as possible by learning new skills, participating on projects, obtaining certifications, meeting new people to network with, whatever it takes. You want to continue to prepare yourself for something better. If the work makes you unhappy, make sure you know how to "turn it off" when you leave for the day—you definitely don't want to bring work issues back to the house.

Other Signs You May Be in a Career Hole

If you can't move up because someone in front of you isn't moving, you are in a career hole and you need to either be OK with the role you are stuck in or be proactive and consider moving into a new role and create your own path. Be careful how this is handled as you don't want to bash your boss; there may be reasons they aren't moving. You also want to make the move as much of a win/win as you can. If you do move, don't leave your old department holding the bag… you never know when you will work with those people again and you want them to have a favorable memory of you.

We're Cool… If there is a group/clique, do not assume you will be able to break into it (honestly, don't even waste your time trying). I've seen multiple people have to leave companies due to their inability to get evaluated fairly as they were not part of the cool kids' group. If you are in this situation, you are in a career hole—stop digging and look for a different path. By the way, this is a difficult thing; there are times the members of this group take care of their own, and by not being part of it you are potentially missing out on opportunities. The cost to be in, however, can be high, and when the members of the group fall out of favor at the company, so will you. Also, don't get dragged into "talking smack" about anyone with this group—be Switzerland and stay neutral. My philosophy is: 1. Don't say anything about someone who is not there to provide their own perspective or defend themselves and 2. If there is a conversation about someone, don't say anything that you wouldn't directly say to the person being talked about. These two things will keep you from being seen as a gossip. When people talk to me about other people, my first thought is… I wonder what they say about me?

If You Work For a Terrible Boss, this is most definitely a career hole. Some people are great at what they do but should never manage people or teams. I've seen so many examples of people who are good at something (an activity or process) be put in charge of that "thing". Being great at writing code or copywriting, sales, accounting, marketing, or analysis doesn't make you a great manager. Having expertise in the area you are going to manage isn't a bad thing, but that alone does not assure someone will be a good manager or leader. If you have a real ding-a-ling for a manager, don't make the mistake I've made on several occasions by trying to wait them out (i.e., eventually the company will realize they are bad and manage them out) rather, start to look for a new path. Nothing good is going to come from working for a bad manager… you will not learn anything (other than how not to manage), you will possibly be guilty by association and you may become unwanted by others since you are part of a poorly run area… who would want to introduce that into their organization?

CHAPTER 45

There Aren't Enough Chairs at the Table

THINK OF ADVANCING IN YOUR CAREER LIKE TRAVELING UP THE side of a pyramid: as it narrows, there are fewer seats at the tables near the top, and as you advance and climb, you need to understand that the competition for the chairs at those coveted tables is going to be more intense.

At lower levels you were likely recognized and promoted for your hard work; at the next level it becomes more competitive, as everyone probably has a strong work ethic and similar background of success, and hopefully all are competent and deserving based on their contributions. Given this dynamic, other factors may now come into play. It could be perception, relationships, bias, department (is it a new, growth or critically important area to the company) ...whatever the reason, at some point, someone is going to be left out.

If there weren't enough chairs for you to get a seat, you may feel slighted, which could motivate you or it may create bad feelings toward the company. One option is to wait for the next opportunity, but if it doesn't happen the next time, it may not ever happen. If you love your work and a promotion would just be the icing on the cake, then no worries—but if you truly want to advance and grow and if it's not happening where you are, it may be time to look for open chairs at someone else's table. It may not be that you're not deserving of the chair; it's just that there may be many deserving people, and not everyone gets a seat.

The good news is, this is within your control. If you choose to stay, don't hold a grudge, that was your choice (you shouldn't hold a grudge anyway, just move on and move forward). The company doesn't "owe" you anything other than a fair wage for the job you are doing. It's not their responsibility to manage your career and assure you are provided the opportunities you think you have earned or deserve. On the flip side, you don't "owe" the company anything other than quality work for your salary. If they don't want to invest in your career, you can leave.

If you do choose to leave, don't burn any bridges; you never know what the future holds—plus it's a pretty small world, and people talk, and there is no reason to damage your reputation. The last job I left was difficult; I really liked my work and I was surrounded by some awesome people, but I wanted to try some other things and couldn't do both. I left on what I believe were good terms—if I ever wanted to go back, they could choose to take me or not. If they didn't want me back, it wouldn't be related to anything unprofessional I did prior to leaving. Don't give an employer a reason to not want you back. Someone from that company may end up working in a different place you are targeting and having left them with a good feeling about you may be what lands you that next job.

For the record, companies don't hate when there is competition, and you shouldn't either. It makes you strive to be better; which is great for the company, especially if there are multiple people trying hard to be their best. It will make the company better and it will make you better. Regardless of what happens, you will be more valuable and marketable because the competition challenged you to grow professionally.

Competition can bring out the best in people, but it can also bring out the worst. Once a competition ends, there may be winners and losers. The winners may not want their fiercest competition around any longer, so they eliminate that role and say goodbye to that person (which may be you). The loser probably won't want to be constantly reminded that they lost, and quite frankly, they can probably be a "winner" somewhere else. Always assume you are competing for that next role, and be ready if you get it, but also be ready if you don't.

CHAPTER 46

Give Me More Money or I'm Leaving

I'VE SEEN PEOPLE WHO WERE NOT ABLE TO OBTAIN RAISES LOOK OUTSIDE the company for opportunities, only to have the current employer match their new pay (offer) when they threaten to leave. This sounds great; you didn't have to leave and still got the raise you wanted, and probably deserved. But what does it say about a company that is only willing to increase your compensation after you threaten to leave?

The company is comprised of people, and the company or its people (i.e., managers) may now have a bias against you and may always have it in the back of their mind that you are unhappy and are a flight risk—they may even try to replace you once they can get someone else up to speed on your role. I'm sure there are companies that don't give this a second thought and are glad they retained you but think it through before you agree to stay for that matching salary. If the culture is the type to hold it against you, it may be better to take the other offer and leave—after all, something made you look elsewhere in the first place. The other consideration is that you just burned a bridge with the company that offered you the new position. This may or may not bother you, but they will definitely remember it. This doesn't mean you shouldn't look, or that you shouldn't leverage another offer to earn more—you should always do what's best for you; companies will certainly do what's best for them. All I am suggesting is to think through the dynamics of the situation and really be prepared to leave if the company calls your bluff.

Speaking of Leaving—I Always Wanted to Live There...

A willingness to relocate provides greater opportunity for growth. It's basic math: if the geography is larger, there will be more potential jobs for you to target. For me, I was willing to move a few times, but eventually landed in an area where we decided to put down some roots—we finally had a house we loved, good neighbors, friends… basically our "network" and a place we called home. I went from Pennsylvania, to Florida, to Tennessee, to Texas and had professional growth each time. After I left my last job, I had offers to return to Pennsylvania and Florida and also had opportunities in Massachusetts, Oklahoma and a couple of other areas outside of Texas, but decided I no longer wanted to relocate; I was in a position where I could make that choice. If I desperately needed a job, I certainly would have considered moving again.

If things aren't working where you are, it may be an opportunity to improve on that. Plus, you potentially start a great new career somewhere else. My personal opinion on this is the younger you are, the easier it is to move—but that's just me. Once you have school-aged kids, it can get a little tougher; they make friends and extended family may be near, and you don't want to upset that dynamic.

Regardless of where I've lived, I've found that I was able to adjust pretty quickly. New towns can be exciting and for the most part, everywhere you go has a lot of the same things. Starbucks and Walmart look the same regardless of which corner of the country you live, and Amazon delivers the same items and doesn't discriminate by zip code. There are definitely some regional things you may miss, and there are some unique cities like New York (Broadway is better than local dinner theater) but for the most part, you'll probably adjust. There can be considerable differences in weather and geography, and you should definitely take this into account. For example, I didn't think I would be able to leave the Florida beaches, but I discovered I also loved the Tennessee mountains—there are definitely tradeoffs to consider. Depending on the state, you will also want to calculate the cost of living, including taxes; this can impact your savings and retirement. If possible, try to negotiate these factors into your salary.

You know yourself better than anyone, so if you have a taste for certain foods or access to a certain culture that you can only get in specific places, you will need to figure out what level of tradeoff is acceptable to you. I guess what I'm saying is this: don't over-think it or be in fear of a relocation more than you need to be. Definitely do your homework, but you may be surprised at how much you enjoy a new town.

Also, a move doesn't have to be forever, you can do it for a while with the plan to move back. Keep in mind, things don't always work out, so you may want to rent first; I've seen people get relocated for a job and then find themselves out of work within a year. Perhaps things didn't work out, the company changed in some way, they were not a good fit for the role or maybe they just missed home. Regardless of the reason, it's easier to rent for a short time to make sure the situation is satisfactory before buying a house. If you don't want to move on a regular basis, one approach is to find a town that has lots of opportunities in your field. If you want to be a deep-sea fishing guide, you shouldn't move to Idaho, as opportunity in this field is likely limited. I'm currently in Texas, and close enough to retirement that I'm not sure we would leave to move somewhere with a state income tax—I would need a pretty big upside tradeoff to make another move… but I never say never.

Here's one final consideration: be honest with yourself. If everywhere you've worked ends in disaster, and you know the problem may be you, then your options can be limited. Consider landing on the low risk side of the equation… in other words, don't relocate and buy a new house when none of your previous jobs lasted more than a year or two. If you've had long steady positions and regular career growth at previous jobs, do your homework when interviewing and take a calculated risk for something better. Unless you are contractually obligated, there is no law that says you can't change your mind and leave.

CHAPTER 47

I Already Know the Answer...

IF YOU ARE A MANAGER AND YOU ASK YOUR TEAM FOR INPUT, MAKE sure it's because you really want it. If you never take any of their suggestions or ideas serious, don't ask. Clearly, you're not always going to take their advice, but when you are simply asking them so it looks like you are being inclusive, you should probably skip the request. Here's why; people like to be engaged in the process and when given an opportunity, also like to have a say about their work. Involving them may generate good feelings, a sense of being included and even greater loyalty. However, if every single time they are asked for their opinion it is dismissed or ignored, the opposite of what was just described may happen; plus, they will stop putting any critical thought into their feedback knowing you have already decided on a course of action basically rendering their input irrelevant.

There will be times when you need to validate your position or want to make sure you have considered all sides of a topic, and hearing others' thoughts can be helpful. If that is the case, share why you are asking for input up front so everyone understands what you are trying to accomplish. Here's another consideration to keep in mind—just because someone doesn't have a title equal to yours doesn't mean they aren't insightful & smart or that their opinions aren't valid. Sometimes their perspective can be the difference when making an important decision.

I've actually lived this, and have had different bosses on both ends of the spectrum. Seeing both sides, I decided a long time ago that whenever I solicit input, I let the person know why I'm asking. Sometimes it's to validate something I've already thought through and just want to see if they arrive at the same conclusion, other times it's because I am "stuck" and needed a fresh or different perspective. I've found when you are honest with someone, for example when I've been stuck, the person you ask for input tends to appreciate the request for assistance. It lets them know you value their opinion, thought process, knowledge and respect them enough to ask for their point of view. This can be empowering for people, and I've found brings out a level of creative and critical thought that may not otherwise be shared.

CHAPTER 48

Titles Are the Same Everywhere...

CTUALLY, THEY ARE NOT. DEPENDING ON WHERE YOU WORK, A VP, for example, may have very different expectations, responsibilities and pay at company A vs. company B. I know many people who came from one company where VP's were actually equivalent to Managers or Directors at another company. Definitely be careful taking that next job if you aren't ready for it. Having a title isn't the same as having experience. Personally, I've never been impressed by titles for this, and many other reasons, but when interviewing for a new role, be honest with yourself before taking that impressive title. I knew a colleague that left the company I was working at to jump two levels in title. They were moving from a medium-sized, privately held company to a large multi-national. They interviewed well and convinced the hiring manager that their current title and level of responsibility were similar to the role they were applying for and were confident they could handle the job. They discovered within two months that they were way out of their depth. Sadly, they were now out of work, their old position back-filled leaving them without a job.

I never think it hurts to talk with someone about another role, and I always believe it's worth taking a calculated risk, but you have to be honest with yourself and know when you are in over your head. This doesn't make you a failure; in fact, it may be what makes you a success.

CHAPTER 49

Stay Relevant to Stay Employed

F YOU ARE A DEVELOPER, KEEP YOUR CODING SKILLS CURRENT. Project managers… stay up to date on the latest certifications. Sales… keep closing new deals or acquiring new clients. Analysts… don't lose your edge and keep learning new techniques and tools. Whatever your vocation, always be learning and improving. I can assure you, the next wave of younger, hungry and cheaper employees is always right around the corner and they're not beat down by the grind of corporate life yet, so everything still seems company-rific to them. For better or worse, once your skills diminish, most companies will find a way to replace you.

I have seen my fair share of what I call relationship retentions… i.e., someone gets to keep their job due to strong relationships at the company. Do not count on this happening for you. While this type of job security is good for the individual, it sucks for someone who can do a better job than them. Obviously, who you know and how you are connected is important and if you are able to pull off the role of "hanger on" (someone who no longer has the skills necessary to do the job but somehow never gets let go) then more power to you; but with limited or diminishing skills your future is tenuous at best. My point here is this: don't give a company any reason to let you go. Once you become expensive, they will be looking for a way… yes, they really will—so do your best to make it hard for them. Keeping your skills current is good for the company, but more importantly, it's good for you. It's difficult to fire competence—assuming it's cheap enough… once it gets expensive, it becomes easier for companies to justify firing even competent people.

If you are reorganized, downsized, quit, fired… or some other form of being let go from your position, there is no need to make a scene. Leave with some class and don't make the company get security involved. Nothing positive will come from making a scene. I've seen both sides of this, and by far, leaving in a dignified way is best. A couple of side notes here:

If you are unlawfully let go and you are given papers to sign, it may be worth having an attorney look them over. You may be surprised that you can afford an attorney for a simple review like this.

The company will likely treat you nicely and may even provide a severance package. They do this because they want you out the door, and with severance usually comes a liability waiver and a lower likelihood of suing for wrongful termination. Whatever it takes to get you out the door and off the property is their goal. Knowing that this is their goal, be sure to ask for severance, extended healthcare, outplacement services, and any other benefits you think are appropriate. The absolute best time to negotiate is early and before you sign anything. Once you've agreed to terms, and especially after you are literally out the door, it is unlikely the company will change their position. The company may become more willing to meet any reasonable separation requests if they are made through an attorney, so if you retain one to review any paperwork, this may be a good time to ask for some of those items that may help provide a "soft landing".

Even if you do sign papers saying you won't sue the company, you may still be able to sue the company. At least this is what several lawyer acquaintances have told me, including one at a company I worked for that utilized such agreements. It may be worth a conversation with an attorney to evaluate your individual situation.

Depending on why you were let go, you may or may not be welcomed back… but definitely don't bank on finding your way back. It would probably make more sense to focus on what's in front of you. One of my favorite cliché sayings is "…don't trip over something behind you."

Even if you fought to get outplacement services, don't get your hopes up on the service being helpful. Some are, some are not; it's really you who will make the difference, not a service. Keep in mind, this service is being paid for by the company that let you go, and the job of the outplacement firm is to do what they need to do to provide the services the company said they would provide, and then to get more business from the company. This is going to sound harsh, but they really don't care about you, as you are just a number and an invoice to generate revenue for them.

Funny story about outplacement services—one of the services I once used scheduled weekly check in meetings for 30 minutes but each one lasted no more than 5-10. They couldn't get through their script quick enough with me; anything to get me off the phone and on to the next client. I had one person provide advice on how to set up a social media profile (i.e. LinkedIn). I suggested that I would look at theirs to help guide my format… they told me they didn't have one. I probably wouldn't ask a vegetarian how to cook a steak… they may know, but I'm not sure I would trust their advice. Use these services where you need help, and if they are helpful… that's a bonus, but don't be surprised or disappointed if they are not.

CHAPTER 50

Be Prepared to Retire at 50!

SERIOUSLY, IF YOU GET LAID OFF IN YOUR LATE 40'S OR AT ANY point in your 50's, you may find it difficult to land another role—at least one that is at a level that will pay you what you are accustomed to. You may also need to relocate for a new job, which is not something everyone can or wants to do. If you find yourself out of work later in life, you can still find another job and have a great end to your career, but as we have all come to learn, life isn't fair and there is no guarantee you will be able to land another role that gets you to retirement, so it's best to be ready.

LinkedIn and other job-related sites are filled with people in their 40's and 50's who thought they would always be employed but are not. They want to be, but the deck is stacked against you once you reach a certain age—it really is. Companies absolutely have an age bias, and don't believe for a minute they won't discriminate against you. I hope this doesn't happen to you, but if it does, you want to be prepared. The good news is that many acquaintances, friends and former colleagues I know who experienced this situation were still able to find a new job. Most of them did it through leveraging their network, reinforcing how important "who you know" is. Spend time keeping your network current and don't just take from it, but also help others in need. You never know when you will be in a similar situation and people may remember your kindness and be willing to assist when you need a hand. Karma shouldn't be underestimated. To be abundantly clear, companies absolutely have an age bias and will discriminate against you, so do your best to be prepared.

A Sad Story About My Father: He retired, and within a year was diagnosed with cancer so for the rest of his life instead of relaxing, golfing and spending time with grandkids, he spent his days going though radiation and chemotherapy treatments. You certainly don't want to retire so early that you run out of money in your twilight years, but you also don't want to work so long that the minute you retire, you die. That's not the final chapter anyone wants. Some people have the luxury of inherited wealth, but many will have to rely on what they have saved and invested on their own. If you fall into the latter category, like I do, you will need to depend on your own savings when you retire. A way to do this is to live, at a minimum within your means, and if you want to save even more, live below your means. I know, I sound like your parents; but it's reality. You also need to understand how social security is calculated, how you will be taxed on 401K, IRA and other retirement accounts when taking distributions. Most of this knowledge is readily available, and if you know how to do math, you can figure it out. If you don't know how to do math, find an affordable financial advisor who will act as a fiduciary and help you define a plan.

Let Me Throw In another Car Story: I think back to some of the cars I wanted to buy and wow, am glad I didn't. Designs change, performance and safety gets better with time, and cars rarely increase in value. I saw a television show a few years back and an older high-end sports car raced a new compact family car. The modern family car was actually faster and won the race. It was loaded with more comfort and safety features than the high-end sports car, too. The point being: think about how you spend your money. Overspending on a single pair of shoes is something you can probably recover from, overspending on a high-end vehicle may be something you come to regret – they are expensive and within a couple of years other, cheaper vehicles will be better equipped, require less maintenance, be safer and will probably even perform better.

Another quick car story… my wife worked at a company that awarded stock to employees as part of the compensation package. At the time, the company was growing exponentially. One of her colleagues cashed out a portion of their stock and bought an awesome new Lexus. This person's colleagues started to track the cost of the car on a whiteboard as the stock continued to split and increase in value. It became a running joke, and at one point I think the "cost" of the car (i.e., what the current value of the stock was) reached close to $350K. They could have bought a pretty nice house for cash… an asset that typically retains or increases in value and had no mortgage payment. Instead, they purchased an expensive car that after a few years was worth a fraction of its original cost. This doesn't mean you shouldn't buy a car. Unless you live in a high traffic city that also provides public or other means of transportation, you will need a way to get around. But what I'm saying is be thoughtful in what you buy and how you spend your money; you are going to need it someday. If you love cars and have a ton of disposable income and more savings than the average bear, get yourself a cool car, just remember: it's always better to save too much than not enough.

From Cars to Houses: Our first house was a new build in a new neighborhood—the size was perfect for what we needed but we discovered the HOA to be lax and after about 10 years, some of the properties in the neighborhood started to fall into disrepair. The city we lived in was also not very interested in providing amenities for the community (at least from our perspective).

Our home was well taken care of and still in great shape, but we saw a broader downward trend of maintenance and care in the neighborhood and decided to move. We didn't live in a slum area by any means - and most of the neighbors directly around us were really nice people. We were going to miss the house and some friends, but made a financial and life decision to buy more house than we needed in order to upgrade our neighborhood. We always say we bought the neighborhood, not the house. The good news is the new neighborhood stays well maintained, but as with any neighborhood, nicer homes don't always mean nicer people. Our old neighborhood had nice people and some ding-a-lings, our new neighborhood has some nice people and some ding-a-lings. The city we moved to is a more community conscious municipality—the additional cost to live there was worth it to us.

Use common sense when spending your money—I can (almost) guarantee you will be glad you did.

CHAPTER 51

Go Work For a Cult (Not Really)

'M NOT GOING TO MENTION THE EMPLOYER, BUT I WORKED AT A place that talked about the iconic founders and how they started the company by working on it as a part-time side project, eventually growing it from nothing into a thriving, multi-national organization. Ironically, my manager knew I had some personal interests that occupied my time away from work and the discussion they had with me was basically this: they wanted me to make the company my priority and expected it to be as important to me as family. Good thing the founder's former organization didn't require such devotion, or this company never would have been created. I probably could have just gone along to get along, but I really didn't want to work somewhere that had a "do as I say, not as I do" culture or thought my job was ever going to be as important to me as family. To be clear, a job is a very important thing, as it provides for your family in many ways, but it is not your family. I've bought into corporate values before only to be disappointed and knew that forced devotion was never going to work for me. So, I moved on. Why companies believe people will forgo family and health for them is a mystery to me... I guess because some people are so desperate for work, they allow a company to take advantage of them?

I wavered about mentioning this next company by name but decided not to—only because I haven't specifically mentioned any other companies I worked for (or with) in this book. For a number of years, I managed a team that implemented, managed, developed, merged and integrated a Customer Relationship Management (CRM) platform. I had understood the technical side very well, I wasn't a hands-on admin or developer, but I could talk to the technical side in an informed way.

As important, or maybe more important, was that I knew the business side and on a regular basis had to justify the cost for additional expansion and growth on the platform. I learned how to tell this business story and became pretty adept at it, and also understood techniques that resonated with the senior executives who made financial investment decisions during budget season. I also managed a sales & business operations group that was responsible for implementing the selling process into the CRM system. In addition, I was responsible for the training team, building reports, integrating with other systems, rolling out collaboration tools, incentive compensation, marketing campaigns, call center knowledge base, and so on. I even hosted several user group and platform supporting events at our corporate headquarters to further the advancement of their user and developer communities.

After leaving that role, I applied for a couple of positions at the company whose platform we utilized, where the requirements of the job openings closely paralleled the work I did. My personal perspective was I would be an ideal person to go into organizations and talk about the value of the platform, help them understand the justification for the investment and grasp how the platform could be leveraged beyond just sales and marketing. Unfortunately, I received rejection letters as quickly as I submitted interest. In more than one example, I even had internal recommendations, only to be rejected without even having a conversation. There are many reasons this could happen… here are a few:

I simply wasn't as qualified as I thought. I guess this is possible but given my decade + working on this and other CRM platforms, it is unlikely.

Someone else was more qualified, which I am fine with; there are a lot of smart people out there…. although the roles stayed posted for weeks, even months, after the immediate rejection letters.

My submittal wasn't automatic screening bot-friendly and was missing all the appropriate key buzz words and catch phrases. I sure miss the days of working with actual humans.

Did the previous employee reps who supported me from that company not paint a positive picture of me in their internal notes? Possible, as I wasn't a push over and didn't empty the company wallet for them; but part of my job was to get a good price on licenses and not expand into areas we didn't need. If this is why I was declined a conversation, that's on them, not me (in fact, I should have been seen as the ideal candidate since I would know how to respond to any pushback, like the kind they used to get from me).

Perhaps they want young people to represent the brand, not well tenured employees. I hope this isn't the case, as I'm pretty sure it's illegal, and the company reportedly has a strong commitment to fairness—especially when it comes to discriminatory practices. Again, I would think having an executive (I was a VP at the time) who once had to help justify the buy decision then implemented, built out and managed a system, would be an excellent choice to have in conversations with other executives now making those same decisions.

I'm not saying this company exercised any bias against me; maybe my submittal was not well written and didn't catch their attention. I do think in general that there is an age bias, either purposeful or unintended, that companies have (again, not specific to this company)—but that's just one person's opinion. I also believe companies want to project an image of a "young and vibrant" workforce. I was (and am) vibrant, but no longer seen as young.

I know quite a few individuals who work at this company and asked them for feedback and insight. More than one mentioned that being deeply connected and active in their online groups would be helpful. "They want to see you are dedicated to the platform," one told me. Well, that is hard. Someone who has targeted multiple companies can't spend all their time dedicated to a single ecosystem in the hopes that it works out—so, I didn't put all my eggs in one basket and perhaps wasn't deeply enough connected. I like how this company is committed to issues like the environment as well some other social stances related to their business practices—I think it would have aligned nicely with my personal value set—but things don't always work out. Frustrating.

I may never know the reason I couldn't even get a conversation with a recruiter or hiring manager—but the wandering path to my point is, sometimes you have to be very committed to something to have it work in your career. I know many people who have done this with various companies. If you are going to navigate one of these paths where your job also becomes your life, make sure it's with an industry leader and that it's something you really want to do. Once you fully commit, it gets more difficult to change paths; it's not impossible, but definitely more difficult.

On several occasions, I wasn't willing to lose my identity by creating a new one that was defined by a company instead of by me— I've done that before and had no interest in doing it again. There are many people who have benefited by going all in on tying their expertise directly to an offering—the company I reference in this section is one of them. I know many who have done great financially, as well as from a career development standpoint, and have become very marketable because of their deep platform commitment. Being marketable is important. If instead of becoming a subject matter expert on this leading platform, you instead picked a niche player, you would likely have limited opportunity. Be aware of the market and give yourself as much opportunity as possible. If you are with a niche company, look for ways to leverage that into a path that allows for more opportunity and marketability. It's possible being an expert in a niche area can be rewarding, especially if you are the only one that has a particular skill, but this is no guarantee of security, and if the company you work for moves to an alternate solution, you may or may not have a role to play; and if no one else uses that niche platform, your opportunities may no longer exist. My feedback is to align yourself with a market leader who provides opportunities in multiple geographies. You never know when you'll need a job.

CHAPTER 52

Is It Still Possible to Look Like a Stand-out Job Candidate?

I N GENERAL, YES; BUT WHAT ABOUT WHEN YOU ARE LOOKING FOR A job on social platforms… can anyone really stand out, for example, on LinkedIn?

Not to brag, but I'm pretty good "in person;" the problem is, it's hard to get to the in-person part of a job interview these days because I look exactly like everyone else on paper (or on the screen, in this case). I think I'm less SEO (Search Engine Optimization) friendly than most, too—likely because I tried to stand out, which ironically got me left out.

The reality is that many roles are only posted because they have to be posted, not because the job is really available. Let's face it, there is probably an internal candidate someone already knows and wants or they have a personal network connection, but because the company either does business with the government or they need to comply with state or federal laws, they post the role, put the ever present and debatable "we don't discriminate" statement at the bottom of the post and let it fly. But let's assume for a minute that it really is a level playing field. How does one differentiate themselves today?

The challenge is everyone has the exact same boxes and fields to fill in, the same format to follow, the same words used to describe themselves and everyone writes the exact same way to try to get noticed by some screening bot behind the scenes. When you do get a screening call with a human, everyone answers every question the same because the entire world is reading the same articles, watching the same videos and using the same script hiring managers and HR pro's say they want and need to hear.

I have been creative with a few of my submittals, but even that has only gotten me a "kudos" note back from a couple of companies saying it was "very creative" or that they "really liked the approach," but as much as they liked the approach, they ultimately decided to go in another direction, likely with someone that they already knew or fit the cookie cutter corporate mold.

I have a blog I rarely update (it's OK, no one really reads it) and the built in "SEO assistant" is never happy with me... my sentences are too long or complex, I have a passive vs. active voice, I use too many conjunctions—you've got to be kidding me—they are easy to understand sentences and it's a blog, not Twitter.

Back to LinkedIn—LinkedIn seems to be becoming more and more like Facebook but instead of trying to BS everyone about how great your home life is with impressive pictures of fancy vacations to exotic places, nice restaurants and over-achieving kids, it provides a similar platform to exaggerate... I mean, highlight how spectacular you are at your job and how great your professional life is. Everyone saved their employer money, improved processes, has made things more efficient, led a team to success, implemented, integrated, managed, met, exceeded, was recognized, innovative, creative, collaborative, etc., etc. It's amazing any companies are still in business after any of us left them. To any recruiters reading this, what exactly is it you are looking for... what makes someone stand out?

Sites like LinkedIn remind me of the hallways at one of my previous jobs. The walls were covered in inspirational posters with one-word messages that need no other grammatical support.

"Perseverance," "Excellence," "Synergy," "Motivation," "Success," "Responsibility," "Discipline," "Honesty," "Ambition," "Embezzling" ... and my favorite "Team"—with all the letters of TEAM capitalized—"Together, Everyone Achieves More." All but one are good positive messages, but not terribly helpful. Just so we are on the same page, embezzling is the one that is not positive, just threw that in to see if you are actually reading.

The LinkedIn platform, like Facebook, leaves one with few, if any other options. If you want to connect, you need to be on the platform but I have found you have limited ability to be creative. The sad part is, no one even wants creativity anymore—only headlines get read, and no one visits external links to more creative content… they really don't. Part of this is because many social platforms frown upon this; they never want a user to click away from their walled in ecosystem. In fact, you could be "penalized" with search ranking and feed positioning if you anger the algorithm.

I once provided some original content, sharing real experiences, which generated considerable traffic and I believe started important conversations. I was rewarded by having my account frozen/locked and my content pulled from feeds (don't anger the ecosystem). As the story goes, I was eventually turned back on, but it felt like unless you sponsor content (i.e., pay) it's difficult to get any significant traction. There are very limited options other than LinkedIn (for business) and sadly, people have become less unique and authentic because they don't want to upset the algorithm, or worse: look like anything less than the perfect candidate. So, now you post another cookie cutter profile trying to impress a computer, and a desire to look perfect instead of real.

If you really need a job, my suggestion is to comply with the algorithm to assure you get included in the vetting process—if you aren't in the mix, you have zero chance. I think it's still OK to be more creative with individual submittals to enhance the cookie cutter profile, but you definitely need to get yourself on to the shortlist; so, regardless of how creative you get with other submittals, be sure to also follow the rules to avoid being excluded. If you really want a fighting chance, it is my belief that the best way to get noticed is to know someone that can introduce or recommend you.

CHAPTER 53

I'm Tired of the Grind, I'm Going to Start My Own Business!

THERE IS ACTUALLY ENOUGH MATERIAL FOR THIS SECTION TO write a separate book, which I may do, but I'll stick to a high-level synopsis for now.

In general, starting your own business can be a very rewarding endeavor, but you better be disciplined and don't think for a second that it's going to be easy or will eliminate the daily grind. In the last corporate job I had prior to starting my business, the organization was being restructured and I was offered a role to stay — it was a different title, but the same pay & benefits. The offer was good, and I really liked what I did, but in the end, I declined. There was something else I was passionate about and wanted to do, but it was going to require a tremendous amount of time to do it and I couldn't have a day job and this new venture at the same time. I knew if I didn't try, I would never do it, so I tried. Here's some of what I learned.

First, do you really want to do this? Seriously, it's freaking hard! The amount of time it takes to start your own business is approximately 1,000X more than you think it will be (that may be a slight exaggeration, but it's a non-stop commitment). Many assume a great idea is worth something - in reality, it isn't... everyone thinks having an idea assures business success. It doesn't. We all have said something like "look at that, someone should build such and such – they would make a fortune." Everyone thinks they have a business idea – the idea part is easy; turning that idea into a business is extremely hard. It's not like "the idea" isn't important; just know that alone is not enough. Imagine the perfect house you would love to build – easy to imagine, hard to build. You can envision the end product, but may not have thought about the foundation, walls, plumbing or electrical, for example… and it's not like you can do electrical before you have walls, or paint before you have a roof. It's an involved, complex process that requires considerable planning.

So, I had an idea… and had been creating the business plan on weekends and had a sense for what I wanted to build. Now I needed to form the company—should it be an LLC, a C Corp., an S Corp…. what is the right answer? Initially, I believed the company may have some foreign investment, so we were going to need a C Corp., but later decided not to take outside investors and landed on an S Corp. It made the most sense from a business and tax perspective. I needed an attorney to do this. The original plan was to reach out to some former colleagues and acquaintances who were attorneys, thinking they may be willing to help me out, but I realized that may be asking a lot of them and I wouldn't have any control over their availability, especially for follow up needs; so, I chose to pay for the service. I found a reasonably priced firm that understood my needs, but it took a while to find them, as rates for attorneys are all over the place. In the end, it wasn't outrageously expensive, but it also wasn't pocket change.

The business itself was going to require an app, so I needed to find a developer. I had pretty extensive experience working with developers from my previous roles and was comfortable that I could evaluate capabilities and find a good organization to work with. The problem is, most of the U.S. based developers were very expensive, so I had to look at outsourcing it overseas. I had some experience working with offshore resources, so I started with some contacts I already knew. They turned out to be more expensive than expected, so I had to start doing research on other options. I found a group in Europe, did some background checking and decided to contract with them. They had experience building apps, good references and their project manager spoke English—a big help when working with offshore resources. I had some experience reviewing contracts but wanted the attorney to review the agreement given it was an international contract. The good news is that we were able to agree on terms and I signed the agreement. More attorney's fees and now a down payment on the development costs.

I got a little ahead of myself; in order to agree to terms with the development company, I needed a quote, so I spent untold hours creating the wire frames of how the app should look and function and provided it to my offshore team to provide a quote. Let's jump ahead a little: the app also had a built-in payment component, so I needed to use a vendor that could securely transact payments in the app—this took weeks to work through. The app sends appointment notifications—this took a while to evaluate and select a vendor. The app needed to work on both Android and iOS, so we had to make a decision on what type of code to use for development. Once the app was completed it needed hours and hours of testing on both Android and iOS. No one in my family had an iPhone or iPad, so there's another expense. I needed a business bank account; that took time. I needed a domain; that took time and money. I needed a website, and decided to learn how to build it myself; that took time and even some money. I needed an account on Apple's App Store and Google Play—you would think working with them would be similar, but they are in fact very different. I needed an account with a company to host the app… you guessed it, time and money (monthly money) I needed to insure the new company (time and recurring annual costs). There were other vendors, expenses, and investments in time too… like Dun & Bradstreet, YouTube, video editing software to learn, logos to create, and conference booth materials to design and order.

At the end of the year I discovered that I was no longer comfortable doing my own taxes, so now there was the expense of an accountant. By the way, when I say all these things took time, I mean it took a LOT of time. I work all the time. Given the time difference between my home in Texas and my Euro developers, I had to have things ready for them Sunday night, so I didn't lose every Monday. When I woke up each morning it was already 2 or 3 in the afternoon for them. Friday's were difficult, as their week was over by the time I woke up. You get the idea. In addition, to promote the business we had to go to conferences (time and money) do roadshows and presentations (time and money) and marketing (time and lots of money).

By the time you launch, you are extremely excited and proud of your work and even more excited to share it with the world. It's a good thing you have this pride and excitement, because no one else will care. I did have a few friends, former colleagues and of course family who were supportive, but do not count on anyone helping you—they may or may not, and no one is going to be remotely as interested or excited about what you are doing as you are. This can be deflating and even depressing—you need to have realistic expectations, but also the resilience to persevere when everything seems to be going nowhere.

Some businesses take off and are immediately successful; basically, it goes viral, while others take considerable time or may not succeed at all (this is a much more likely scenario). You will wonder if your business is going to be super successful and change an industry, or simply just fade away.

The point here is this: don't expect immediate success starting your own business, don't think you will have an easier schedule (it's actually worse) don't expect to generate revenue on day 1, whatever you estimated as expenses… double it and don't expect people to be helpful. The people most interested in my business are other businesses selling services related to SEO, marketing, web design, accounting, conferences, insurance, lending, legal support and sales professionals. The other "interested parties" are people who wanted to suggest ways for me to spend money to grow the business. I had many people who tried to convince me to give them partial ownership and in return they would give me zero money, but would offer "free" advice on how to spend my money. None of these people were in the industry I was in, and I could not see how their involvement was going to benefit the business, so I passed on these very gracious offers. If the right person/people were available, I very well may have embraced this approach. For example, if they were influential in the industry, or were able to make introductions or open new doors for the business, this approach may have made sense, but these individuals were not interested in being actively involved. If I was going to take on any partners, they needed to be committed to the business, not a passive observer that was hanging around "just in case" I was successful. If all that hasn't scared you, there is some data that suggests a middle-aged person starting their own business will have a much more difficult time reentering the work force if things don't work out, so be fully informed before you charge down this path. Another piece of advice - start as early as you can, as it may take time to develop; and if possible, do it "on the side" initially so you continue to generate income with your salary while allowing you to determine if it's going to work or not.

Some basic research has shown that the consumer market for the business I created is tremendous, but the provider side of the market I targeted has proven slow to embrace change and didn't understand the consumer shift in their industry (or I didn't understand how dug into tradition this industry was). There are some existing independent providers of the service I built that have been very successful on a small scale, but they are not the status quo. We found that these individual providers are so busy they often turn down new clients, which kind of validates the need identified in our business case. Even when all data points to, and suggests success, it is never guaranteed.

Some traditionalists in this industry bristle when we share the concept. They think we are suggesting they switch to this new model full-time, when what we are actually suggesting is enhancing their existing model using a new approach to engaging customers to supplement their revenue stream and grow their client base.

I want to end this chapter by telling you we were a resounding, industry changing success, but I can't. We did make headway and were starting to generate interest, then the pandemic brought everything to a screeching halt. Just my luck, the two things we didn't plan for were Zombie apocalypse and deadly world-wide pandemic… who would have guessed. Starting your own business can be extremely exciting and rewarding… and humbling and soul crushing. I'm pretty sure I mentioned this, but it's worth mentioning again — life is going to throw you curve balls, don't ever expect it to treat you fairly. This reiterates the importance of having saved your money so you can weather "life isn't fair" storms when they show up.

SECRET HIDDEN BONUS CHAPTER

I'm Selfish, But It's OK Because I'm Important

Just me complaining ...thanks for reading this far!

OK, THIS IS A REAL PET PEEVE OF MINE: DRIVING A VEHICLE while distracted is selfish, and even criminal in many places. If you want to put yourself in danger, I'm sure there is an endless list of other dangerous activities you can go do, but you have no right to make that choice for others. When you are behind the wheel and doing everything but driving, those actions can have a ripple effect on others around you. Your drifting from lane to lane, traveling at a slow speed in a passing lane, sitting still at a green light—are all super dangerous.

When you are at a red light and it turns green but you don't go because you are otherwise occupied, you have altered the course of everyone behind you. Realizing the light has changed and speeding to catch the car in front of you after it's a quarter mile up the road doesn't make everything OK and doesn't change the fact that everyone else is still going to miss the light. Not only did you impact those people, but now the people piling in behind them are going to have to wait for multiple light cycles to make it through. What about that one person who needed to get home for something important and are now going to be late, and maybe make a family member late... now causing an argument… all because you had to put an emoji on something. Or, that person who would have easily made the light but is now uncertain but tries to make it anyway but fails to and gets T-boned at the intersection. Whew, the driver is OK, but the kid in the back seat has a broken leg, or worse. Does that text you were looking at seem important now? There's an old saying about how missing a bus can change your life—same thing here. Be present when driving—know what's going on around you. The machine you are operating is capable of killing someone if not handled responsibly. I know you think it can't happen to you and I can guarantee there are thousands of others that thought the same thing, only to have it happen to them.

Along with children that may be in other vehicles, there are also people whose families depend on them. They are the breadwinner and provider of a mortgage, food, healthcare… everything.

Maybe you think nothing bad will happen to you…until it does. You go from being a big shot that has to be on their device every second, to someone who killed a child, a parent, a spouse and are now maybe headed to prison. Do you really think whatever that thing you were looking at and distracted by was worth it… and did it really need an immediate response?

With few exceptions, whatever you were looking at could have waited, and if something is urgent, simply find an exit or parking lot and pull over. If the issue is that important, it deserves your full attention, anyway. Why should everyone else have to drive defensively due to your selfishness? As important as you may be, you probably aren't as important as you think you are and just about everything can wait for 60 seconds until you can pull over safely.

Data doesn't lie, distracted driving is dangerous and shouldn't be done—so don't be an asshole, just pay attention to what you are doing when you get behind the wheel of a vehicle.

And take your grocery cart back to the corral or store at the supermarket, and don't put your calls on speaker in public… like on a plane or in a lobby, and stop at stop signs, and pick up after your dog, and don't take a call at a concert…on speaker… during the concert, and if you are driving behind me don't merge onto the highway before me and then block me from merging, and stop spitting your gum onto the ground in the parking lot, and control your kids in public—it's not my job to supervise them… sorry, I got a little wound up there.

ABOUT THE AUTHOR

Don's journey took him from blue collar laborer to executive to entrepreneur. He shares his experience and stories in an unambiguous and humorous way to try to help others avoid missteps he's made. When not working on his business, or donating money to the stock market, he likes being involved in community-based efforts to help improve the environment and supports organizations and activities that promote animal advocacy.

Don has an undergraduate business degree as well as an MBA and several certifications related to process improvement. He is married, lives in Texas, considers himself a jack of all trades and master of many and has accepted his rank of "least important" in his home, positioned considerably below the cat.

Learn more at: www.donfesh.com

www.ingramcontent.com/pod-product-compliance
Lightning Source LLC
Chambersburg PA
CBHW022037190326
41520CB00008B/609